TAKE TWO AND NUDGE

The newest safe-sex craze to [...] Packets," which contain a pow[...] experience lasting three to fiv[...]

IS THERE A CLEO AWARD FOR BAD TASTE?

Five San Francisco ad agencies put together an exhibition less than a year after the devastating Loma Prieta earthquake of 1989. The front of their invitation read: "See the kind of work you do when every ad could be your last." Inside was a photo of the mangled Nimitz freeway, which collapsed during the quake.

FORGIVE ME, FATHER, FOR I'VE BEEN REALLY GNARLY

Father Bruce Osborn, pastor of Our Lady of Guadalupe Church in L.A., carries a surfboard in his Jeep, wears cutoffs and T-shirts when he's off duty, and surfs whenever he can find the time. His parishioners call him "Father Rad."

BOW-WOW-LY HILLS 90210

Lassie needed new digs, so a Beverly Hills interior design firm built a two-story doghouse complete with murals, antique bookcases, and photos of Rin Tin Tin and Flipper.

IT SEEMED A-PEELING AT THE TIME

The University of California at Santa Cruz's mascot is the banana slug.

LOONY TOMBS

Epitaph on Mel Blanc's gravestone: "That's All, Folks!"

JANET HEARNE is a Southerner who was temporarily trans-planted to California ("the only place in the U.S. weirder than the South"). She lives in Jonesborough, Tennessee.

JANET HEARNE

ONLY IN CALIFORNIA

FABULOUS FACTS, WEIRD HAPPENINGS,
AND ECCENTRIC EPHEMERA FROM
AMERICA'S MOST ALTERED STATE

A PLUME BOOK

PLUME

Published by the Penguin Group
Penguin Books USA Inc., 375 Hudson Street,
New York, New York 10014, U.S.A.
Penguin Books Ltd, 27 Wrights Lane, London W8 5TZ, England
Penguin Books Australia Ltd, Ringwood, Victoria, Australia
Penguin Books Canada Ltd, 10 Alcorn Avenue, Toronto, Ontario, Canada M4V 3B2
Penguin Books (N.Z.) Ltd, 182–190 Wairau Road, Auckland 10, New Zealand

Penguin Books Ltd, Registered Offices:
Harmondsworth, Middlesex, England

First published by Plume, an imprint of New American
Library, a division of Penguin Books USA Inc.

First printing, July, 1993

1 3 5 7 9 10 8 6 4 2

Ⓟ REGISTERED TRADEMARK—MARCA REGISTRADA

Library of Congress Cataloging-in-Publication Data
Hearne, Janet.
Only in California : fabulous facts, weird happenings, and
eccentric ephemera from America's most altered state / Janet Hearne.
p.   cm.
Includes bibliographical references
ISBN 0-452-27002-2
1. California—Miscellanea.   2. Curiosities and wonders—
California—Humor.   3. Curiosities and wonders—California—
Anecdotes.   I. Title.
F861.5.H43   1993
979.4—dc20   92-42705

Printed in the United States of America
Set in Garamond Light & Gill Sans Condensed

Designed by Steven N. Stathakis

BOOKS ARE AVAILABLE AT QUANTITY DISCOUNTS WHEN USED TO PROMOTE
PRODUCTS OR SERVICES. FOR INFORMATION PLEASE WRITE TO PREMIUM
MARKETING DIVISION, PENGUIN BOOKS INC., 375 HUDSON STREET, NEW
YORK, NEW YORK 10014.

CONTENTS

ACKNOWLEDGMENT

A very special thank-you to John Grimes for his wonderful illustrations and for sharing his vision of life in California.

ONLY IN CALIFORNIA

INTRODUCTION

Why this book?

If I really think about it, and I guess I should since they're paying me, my love affair with California began when I was in the single digits. One of my first cognitive TV experiences was "Route 66." I remember vowing—if a six-year-old can do such a thing—that someday I would travel Route 66 to California. This first vow led to others: In the sixties, under the influence of Brian Wilson and the Beach Boys, I vowed to become a surfer; later, I wanted to be a Haight-Ashbury flower child.

The seventies belonged to Jackson Browne, and although I was getting a little too old for this sort of thing, I promised myself (weakening resolve) that someday I would move to the Coast, meet Mr. Browne, and live happily ever, etc.

During the eighties, I had a falling out with California. I held the state personally responsible for the Reagan years and wanted nothing to do with it. (It also gave us Richard Nixon, but during the Nixon regime I was too enamored with lava lamps and incense to hold a grudge.)

In the nineties, I finally made it; I had the opportunity to live in Los Angeles. The California of my dreams, however, was long dead. Route 66 no longer existed, Brian Wilson had been usurped by his daughters, and as for Jackson, I had, unfortunately, begun to look at life realistically.

When I arrived in California, I expected hippies and head shops; instead I got yuppies and doggie day care. I don't know why I expected the California of my adolescent dreams to stand still while the rest of us got older. Now I see: California was my Never-Never Land.

Evidence to the contrary, this book is a love letter to the Golden State, an effort to preserve (no matter how silly) the memory of the last refuge of the priceless individual. Unfortunately, California itself is an endangered species. So while we have it, let's celebrate its idiosyncracies and rejoice in its oddities—good and bad.

We can all learn from California and try to do better.

Before you begin, however, let me issue a disclaimer. Like Will Rogers, "All I know is what I read in the paper." I have made little or no effort to follow up on news items culled from a vast array of periodicals. If there was an error in the original article, that error may have been unwittingly, or lazily, however you want to look at it, perpetuated here. This book is fun, folks. It's not a scholarly treatise. It is, you might say, a lot like California.

ODDBALLS AND

INNOVATORS

THERE'S SOMETHING ABOUT LIVING AT THE EDGE OF THE earth that makes people, how shall I say this without inviting a lawsuit, unique. When you can go in only one direction (crib note for surfers: that's *away* from the water), your options seem greatly limited and you start casting about back and forth for ways to extend your boundaries. There's up, which explains the platform heel phenomenon of the early seventies; there's down, which does not explain the platform heel phenomenon of the early seventies; and there's out, meaning fat, which is against the law in California. Therefore, many Californians turn inward, and, finding no one home, they become, uh, unique.

They start collecting things. These things can be almonds resembling Rula Lenska, meat scraps that spell out messages from the gods, or maybe green beans that look like Ted Danson without his toupee. Granted, such behavior is a little off, but it's tolerable, and, after a heavy dose of L.A. or San Francisco, cool, refreshing.

But then there's Gumby. For some unexplained reason, and rest assured someone at Stanford is studying this phenomenon as we speak, Californians in large and unnatural numbers are Gumby collectors. You will find Gumby in the poshest beach homes, in the poshest limousines, and in the poshest Beverly Hills mansions. No one collects art anymore —they collect Gumbys. Personally, I think it's time someone stood up and said, "GUMBY IS A DOLL, DAMN IT, AND YOU ARE ACTING LIKE IMBECILES!" (Note: *I* didn't say that, I said "someone" should say that. If I said that, I would be Z-listed, which would mean that from now on I would find myself at Hollywood parties with Danny the Dancing Dog and Phoebe the Wonder Horse.)

Okay, it isn't just the sheer numbers of Gumbys that upset me so. It's more the way Californians display them. They don't place Gumbys innocuously throughout the house; they don't line them up neatly in glass cases. They pose Gumbys. Those little flexible arms can be arranged in a thousand adorable ways.

Here's Gumby leaning nonchalantly against the fireplace, here's Gumby carving the Thanksgiving turkey, here's Gumby clinging to the flush handle of the toilet. The effect is cloying, it is obnoxious, it is enough to make one want to rip off Gumby's flat little head.

To my way of thinking, there is only one thing worse than Gumby purists (those who collect only Gumby figures), and that's Gumby generalists. These weirdos collect Gumby AND his little horse Pokey.

Imagine, if you will, the effect of Gumby posed with Pokey: Gumby riding Pokey by the fireplace, Gumby riding Pokey through the oyster dressing, Gumby riding Pokey to their deaths after I pry them from the toilet handle and throw them into the great porcelain whirlpool.

At this point, I am usually asked to leave. Those who don't ask, just point toward the door, their features contorted with rage, their plumbers' numbers clutched in their fists. I leave, embarrassed but undaunted, and almost always hungry. If only I could control myself until *after* Gumby carves the turkey.

IIIIIIIIIIIIIIIIIIIIIIIIIIIIIIIIIIIIIIIIIIIIIIIIIIIIIIIIIIII

POLITICS MAKES STRANGE BEDFELLOWS, THEY SAY, BUT

in California strange bedfellows make for some mighty strange politics. Consider this cast of characters:

- Elijah Anderson Omega, Palmdale, 1992 presidential candidate, who, if elected, would have made sex illegal for females under eighteen years of age.
- Kip Lee, Redding, was another presidential hopeful. His platform included promises to help bring about the second coming of Christ and to release four space aliens who are being held by the U.S. government in Dayton, Ohio. The aliens, Lee says, have been held captive for forty years.
- Elisha Shapiro was the 1988 Nihilist Party candidate for president. His slogan: "I don't believe in anything. Why do you?"
- At the local level, San Jose has Danny Zezzo, who ran for mayor. Zezzo is also known as the "Boss of Buff," a nickname given to him by *Playboy* magazine. Zezzo was the promoter of Ms. Nude America pageants in the eighties and now has a talent agency, Dancers A La Carte. A La Carte's specialty: nude and seminude performers. Ac-

cording to Zezzo, however, he is proudest of being the first person to get San Jose mentioned in *Playboy*. Unfortunately for Mr. Zezzo, San Jose did not appreciate his cultural contributions and chose not to elect him.

Another mayoral candidate, Terri Pohrman, was described as a "transsexual Brigitte Nielsen lookalike." Miss Terri, as she is called, ran for mayor of Yountville in Napa County. She had a sex change operation in the seventies and so chose for her campaign slogan: "The Change Will Do You Good." If elected, Miss Terri promised to buy "pink lifeboats for everyone."

In 1991, standup comic Tom Ammiano took office as a commissioner on the San Francisco Board of Education. Ammiano is well qualified for the job: He has his master's degree in special ed and for years taught kids with disabilities. In the wake of the Mapplethorpe controversy, as part of his standup routine, Ammiano suggested a Mapplethorpe primer: "Look, look, Jane. Dick!"

This candidate speaks for himself: "I can't articulate it. God, if I could I would love it. But you know that's something I guess I'm going to have to learn, is how to throw that articulation out."—Sonny Bono, Palm Springs mayor and 1992 candidate for U.S. Senate

CHERYL LANDERS TRIED TO MAKE IT AS A CITY BUS DRIVER

in Sacramento, as a nurse's aide, and as a real estate agent before she realized that she should go with her talent: screaming. For $75.00 Landers dresses as the Grim Reaper and delivers screaming telegrams. What, you are undoubtedly asking, is the appropriate occasion for such a service? Landers has worked for people who have quit their jobs and spouses who have quit their marriages. She also screams, offscreen, for the movies.

▌▌

BUST DUSTERS CLEANING SERVICE FEATURES UNIFORMED

maids, but the uniform isn't much—high heels, fishnet stockings, G-strings, and itty-bitty lace aprons. The company, run by men (of course), charges $125 for one and a half hours of cleaning. The maids get $30 plus tips.

▌▌

A SAN FRANCISCO MAN HAS THE WORLD'S LARGEST COL-

lection of Smiley faces. His one-thousand-item collection includes a Smiley-face condom and a Smiley-face toilet brush. Experts say we can thank San Francisco for the Smiley Face itself. It was created by a San Francisco button collector. Now if we can just find the guy responsible for "Have a nice day!"

▌▌

THE 1990 HEAD OF L.A.'S LARGEST HOMELESS SHELTER

likened herself to a corporate executive and said that helping the homeless was a "growth industry." She also liked the corporate lifestyle, so she drove a Mercedes-Benz, wore designer clothes, and received an $85,000 annual salary. Some critics

didn't understand her philosophy, however, and griped when she spent $5,000 on planters and plants, and an additional $200 a month for fresh flowers—to decorate the shelter, of course. The shelter also paid for her car phone and City Club membership dues. The club was necessary for "networking," she said, and she had to have a car phone because she didn't have a beeper.

THE COURT OF HISTORICAL REVIEW AND APPEALS IN SAN

Francisco meets periodically to decide weighty issues. In 1991, the group declared Groucho Marx an official member of Phi Beta Kappa. The group has also determined that the Maltese Falcon lives.

A GROUP OF CITIZENS IN ROSS HAS FORMED THE CALI-

fornia Depopulation Commission, which encourages nonnative Californians to leave the state. The commission thinks that all interstate freeway off-ramps should be removed and has designated August as "Florida Appreciation Month," reasoning that without Florida California would have even more people.

A JESUIT PRIEST AT AN L.A. CHURCH MISSION RAISED OVER

$39,000 to start a day care center for underprivileged children by appearing on "Jeopardy!" His strongest category: Beatles songs.

AFTER A NIGHT OF HEAVY DRINKING, A BELL GARDENS

couple awoke to find their eight-month-old daughter missing. The couple told the police that they were so drunk the night before they couldn't remember if the baby was in her crib when they returned home or if they had left her at a taco stand they had visited around 4:00 A.M. Four days later the baby was recovered in Tijuana. She had been left in a box on a stranger's doorstep. How she got to Tijuana remains a mystery.

FOR OVER TWENTY YEARS, NELVOLIA COLLINS FROM
Carson has kept a Louisiana swamp alligator in her back yard.
The six-foot-long, eighty-five-pound alligator, named Papa, is
a neighborhood pet, and, according to Nelvolia, "has the prettiest eyes you've ever seen."

THE INTERNATIONAL FLAT EARTH SOCIETY, BASED IN
Lancaster, has eleven thousand members who believe that man
never made it to the moon. According to society members,
the July 1969 television broadcast of "One giant step for mankind" was a government and media collaboration to dupe the
world.

JOHN A. KOSTOPOULOS, WHO LIVES IN THE MOJAVE DES-
ert, paints portraits on toilet seats. He started the hobby during
World War II when his toilet seat rendering of Hitler proved
to be popular with his fellow servicemen. Kostopoulos now
has over four hundred painted toilet seats on display in his
front yard. His neighbors (and yes, there are neighbors in the
Mojave Desert), needless to say, are less than thrilled.

IN HONOR OF THE MUCH-BALLYHOOED UMBRELLA PROJ-

ect by environmental artist Christo, Ed Balder, a Lancaster radio personality, set out 1,830 cocktail umbrellas in front of a Mervyn's Center Store. Christo's project cost millions and resulted in one death. Balder's umbrellas cost $57 and were composted after the exhibition.

HOLLYWOOD ARTIST MARK SCHILDER PAINTED A FOUR

hundred-square-foot mural in his studio that included portraits of Madonna, Cher, Farrah Fawcett, and George Burns. Schilder asked for and got the celebrities to provide their personal toothbrushes, which are now pasted alongside the likenesses.

L.A.'S JOB FACTORY, A TEMPORARY EMPLOYMENT

agency, specializes in offbeat assignments. Workers have looked after hot tubs, inspected caskets, sorted tropical fish (bottom up from still moving), chauffered strippers, and dressed as cupcakes.

SUE BUTNER, OF LA VERNE, RUNS A BABY-NAMING SER-

vice. For a small sum, Butner helps couples who are afraid of mislabeling their children. She cautions parents about unfortunate initials such as RAT and names other kids will make fun of, and offers nouveau spellings—an extra vowel or consonant—for traditional names. Butner's service is not limited to new babies. She also helps actors pick stage names and helps authors name their characters.

ARNOLD SPRINGER, A VENICE BEACH ACTIVIST DEVOTED

to controlling development of his community, received $200,000 from a developer to create the Ulan Bator Foundation. Named after the capital of Mongolia, the foundation will educate the public about "Mongolian life and culture by focusing on Mongolian concepts of space, light, air, horizon, physical, popular and spiritual culture." Springer is also distinguished by the skirts he wears, which, he says, "make me happy."

TIMOTHY DUNDON, FORTY-SEVEN, OF ALTADENA,

marched in Pasadena's Doo-Dah Parade, an annual spoof of the esteemed Rose Bowl parade, with his pet yam.

TWINS BLAIR MICHAEL RIKIO IWAMOTO AND HIS

brother Brooks Glenn Joji Iwamoto are unique by virtue of their birth. The boys, born minutes apart at the Tarzana Regional Medical Center, were born in different decades. Blair came along at 11:59 P.M. on December 31, 1989, and Brooks arrived at 12:01 A.M. on January 1, 1990.

BY THE TIME HE WAS FIVE YEARS OLD, GREGORY SCOTT

of Tarzana had made four films, and he had appeared on "Entertainment Tonight" and "Arsenio Hall." Gregory's first film, made at age four with a video camera, was *Pete and Sandy*, about the family dogs. Three more followed: *Secret Treasure, Ghost Camp-Out in the Cemetery*, and *Rock and Roll Teddy Bear*. When Universal Studios executives met the boy, they offered him a five-year contract (which means he'll be in fifth or sixth grade when the contract runs out). For his first project, Gregory will direct two segments of a Universal special.

IN ORDER TO WIN A PAIR OF SUPER BOWL TICKETS, A

North Hollywood man allowed KLOS-FM deejays Mark and Brian to shave his head and decorate his bald pate with Silly String while he soaked in a barrel of ice. His comment on the ordeal: "You only live once."

██

FORGET SISKEL AND EBERT. SAN PEDRO'S RAWLAN

(Tank) Nelson, who has seen more than six thousand films, is the man to trust when it comes to movies. For those who can't drop in on his morning critique at a local coffeehouse, Nelson scribbles his picks on a chalkboard that hangs outside his second-floor window. Passersby stop to look, and area theaters notice an increase in ticket sales for the films Nelson plugs.

██

FATHER MAURICE CHASE OF LOS ANGELES IS AN ADVO-

cate for the homeless, one dollar at a time. Chase collects money—up to $1,500 a week—from celebrities like Frank Sinatra and doles it out to the homeless. Each person receives a dollar to do with as he pleases. In a five-year period, Chase estimates he has handled over five hundred thousand one-dollar bills. In appreciation for Frank Sinatra's generous contributions to Father Chase's efforts, nearly three thousand homeless people signed a Valentine's Day card for the singer. The card read: "One heart simply isn't enough to hold our feelings for you."

██

EARLY IN 1992, IT WAS DISCOVERED THAT HAWTHORNE'S

City Clerk, Patrick E. Keller, who had been collecting a $600-a-month salary from the city for over ten years, no longer lived in Hawthorne. Actually, he didn't even live in California. Okay, to tell you the truth, the man did not live on this continent: He lived in Hawaii. Cornered city officials said Keller was not acting illegally—the law stated only that the city clerk must be a registered voter—but they understood how the voting public might be a bit peeved. Keller's resignation was accepted shortly thereafter.

GOD TOLD NOAH TO BUILD AN ARK, HE TOLD MOSES TO

lead his people out of Egypt, and He told Bob Haifley of Covina to build a life-size statue of Jesus out of toothpicks. The message came in 1986 while Haifley was driving his truck in San Dimas. He accepted the challenge and spent five years and sixty-five thousand toothpicks completing the job. When it was done, Haifley hung the figure of Jesus in front of his garage door and put a spotlight on it. His sixteen-year-old neighbor's reaction to the project: "Whoa!"

LUCY PEARSON, SIXTYSOMETHING, IS THE HUBCAP QUEEN

and her town, Pearsonville, is the Hubcap Capital of the World. In 1959, Lucy and her husband founded the town in the desert off US 395; she began collecting hubcaps that year. Lucy now has eighty thousand hubcaps, some of which she makes into clocks.

CLIFFORD FIELDS AND HIS WIFE, CHRISTINE, LIVED IN A

San Carlos condo with their pet rats. They loved the little darlings so much that they let the rodents sleep in their bed. When the Fieldses left the condo in November 1989, they took three rats with them. The rest they left behind. By March, the remaining rats and their progeny had eaten through the walls into their neighbors' apartments. Humane Society officials removed 295 rats from the condo.

THE SOCIETY FOR SECULAR ARMAGEDDONISM IN SAN

Francisco sponsors the Hotline of Doom, which offers "news and information on the coming Apocalypse." In 1992, the hotline commented on the Rio de Janeiro Earth Summit: "an extremely rare chance for the human race to embarrass itself in front of the rest of the planet." The Society describes itself as "the world's only non-religious group currently monitoring and resisting the approaching Apocalypse." Though it may be resisting, the Doom message concludes with, "And don't forget: It's totally hopeless. Don't give up."

BILLIE HART, SEVENTY-TWO, IS A PIG PROMOTER. HER

"World of Pigmania" exhibit at the L.A. County Fair includes items pigs give their all for: beer cans, crayons, photographic film, gum, erasers, cassette tapes, air freshener. "If you're a pig," Hart said, "there's life after death. Long after they're gone, they go on serving." Hart's card reads: "There's More than Meats the Eye."

LAW AND (DIS)ORDER

ON A PROMOTIONAL TRIP TO TOKYO, LOS ANGELES MAYOR
Tom Bradley tried to reassure the Japanese that L.A. was a "safe city" and that all those stories about gang wars and drive-by shootings were nothing more than myth. "I can tell you with authority," Bradley said (meaning his assistant's assistant got this information from the second cousin of his brother's wife who once drove through Compton), "when there is a drive-by shooting—and they do occur from time to time [oh, about every sixteen seconds, we'd guess]—in no case will you have found that those involved or threatened tourists."

The Japanese were so relieved to hear that gang members check license plates before they off someone, they decided to develop a new California theme park. They're calling it "Crips and Bloods World." The idea is to bring the gangs into the park and let them fight it out. Tourists—who ARE NOT INVOLVED—can experience drive-by shootings firsthand while riding shotgun in a Bloods bumper car, or witness a knife fight while spinning in a teacup. The duck shoot will now be the Crips shoot, using Uzis instead of toy rifles. If you win, you get a free tattoo.

This theme park comes none too soon, since California has lost one of its main draws for the Japanese. Because of the state's reputation as a crime capital, a Japanese businessman brought his wife to California in order to have her murdered. He reasoned that there were so many murders in the state no one would notice another one. Before he was arrested, California travel agencies were even organizing "Bag Your Wife" tours. The package included airfare (a one-way ticket for the wife), hotel accommodations, and a tastefully prepared "Last Supper"—after which a crazed gunman would burst into the room, steal the wife's wedding ring, and blow her away. The tour wasn't a total loss, however; park organizers are now trying to work it into a ride for Crips and Bloods World. Don't believe me? Hey, I tell you this "with authority."

A KINDER, GENTLER LAPD? MATTHEW MCCARTER JUMPED

off the fifty-two-story Southern California Gas Company building in downtown L.A. It is fortunate for McCarter—and for pedestrians below—that he was wearing a parachute. Police gave the thirty-one-year-old man a lecture on "the dangers of parachuting off buildings," told him that he was a "drain" on L.A.'s resources, and released him.

||||||||||||||||||||||||||||||||||||||||||||||||||||||||||||||||

FROM A *SAN FRANCISCO CHRONICLE INDEX* NEWS SUM-

mary: "An initiative aimed at preventing the California Legislature from meddling in the initiative process is expected to be approved for the November 1990 ballot. It would require a vote of the people to approve any change to the state's initiative law." Huh?

||||||||||||||||||||||||||||||||||||||||||||||||||||||||||||||||

GARFIELD PARK WAS AN IDEAL COMMUNITY—GOOD

schools, a lovely park, quiet, calm—until the twins from hell moved to the neighborhood. According to police reports, the two eighteen-year-old boys and their friends blasted tapes of Guns 'N' Roses at all hours, shouted obscenities, urinated on the neighbors' lawns, smashed beer bottles, and raced their cars up and down the street. When the neighbors complained, their property was vandalized. Children could no longer play outside, people lost sleep, sometimes the noise was so loud they couldn't hear their TV sets. During the summer of 1990, Santa Rosa police racked up 160 hours of overtime trying to deal with the problem. When the mother was approached about her sons, she said she couldn't punish her boys, she was afraid of them.

CONVICTED KILLER RICHARD WILLIAM GARRISON SOUGHT

to have his death sentence overturned on the grounds that he did not receive fair representation because his attorney was drunk during the trial. The attorney in question was arrested for drunk driving on the way to the courthouse with a blood alcohol level of 0.27—over twice the legal limit. A trial bailiff remarked after the trial that the attorney's breath "always smelled of alcohol." When asked if he thought the attorney was drunk during the trial, the bailiff said he didn't know because the attorney "always seemed to act the same."

TWO MEN ROBBED A DISNEY STUDIOS PRODUCTION OF-

fice. When asked to confirm the amount of money stolen, Sgt. Don Goldberg of the Burbank police declined to be specific, offering only this statement: "Mickey Mouse is crying."

THE DAY AFTER TWENTY-THREE PEOPLE WERE MUR-

dered by a crazed gunman in Texas, John Murset of Arcadia reported to work wearing camouflage gear and an ammunition belt strapped across his chest. After frantic workers called the police, the courtyard was cleared and the building was searched. Confronted by police, Murset explained that he had been deer hunting that morning and had not had time to change. No charges were filed, but the police told Murset he "could have used a little better judgment."

A SAN FRANCISCO TAXI DRIVER WHO RAN DOWN A MUG-

ger and used his cab to keep him pinned against a wall until police could arrive was ordered to pay the mugger nearly $25,000 for using excessive force. The mugger's attorney said, "I do not think it is fair to take a four-thousand-pound cab and ram someone against a wall."

THE LAPD, ONCE REVERED, IS NOW REVILED BY THE NA-

tion. A float in the Lake Bluff, Illinois, July 4th parade featured two LAPD cop lookalikes duking it out with Zsa Zsa Gabor in front of their black-and-whites.

"PAT, I'LL TAKE THE VASE FOR $220,000." IN ONE IN-

credible shopping spree, a twenty-two-year-old Orange County girl spent the $1 million her mother had embezzled from an employer. The girl bought a Mercedes, a Porsche, a Saab, and a Jeep Cherokee, threw a $10,000 Christmas party, then used $1000 address books to record the names of her new friends.

Christmas tree ornaments and tinsel to trim the house cost another $8,000. In one trip to a shopping plaza, she spent $100,000 on everything from designer sheets (which she later had tailored) to leather coasters. The girl needed four storage units to hold her haul. Police finally caught up with her just before she closed the deal on a $488,000 house.

DETECTIVES CALLED TO A VENTURA COUNTY CANYON

to investigate the death of a twenty-four-year-old woman developed itchy welts. An entomologist ID'd the perpetrator, a rare chigger whose habitat was confined to a one-half-mile area that included the site of the girl's murder. A man questioned about his involvement in the killing said he had been nowhere near the scene of the crime. Police knew he was lying when they discovered he had chigger bites identical to theirs. The man was later convicted of first-degree murder.

A SANTA CLARITA FAST-FOOD WORKER WAS KIDNAPPED

and robbed as she left work to deposit the night's receipts but escaped by jumping from the moving car. When the restaurant higher-ups heard about the crime, they suspended her from her job because she had not deposited the receipts earlier in the afternoon.

JAIE BRASHAR, AKA SYBIL ST. JAMES, AKA SYBIL PARKING,

aka Genevieve Marsden, found a way to make a living without working. She advertised alley kittens as purebreds and sold them for hundreds of dollars to clients unschooled in the fine points of catdom. She met her match in Terry Peterson, who paid $230 for a "Burmese" kitten. When he took it to the vet the next day, he was told the kitten was far from pedigreed. In fact, Peterson learned he could have picked up the same kitten for nothing. When Brashar refused to return his money, Peterson set up a sting of his own. He arranged to have a friend from his acting class purchase two "Angora" kittens from Brashar. He videotaped the whole thing, and just as the transaction was completed, Torrance police arrested Brashar and charged her with attempted grand theft.

||||||||||||||||||||||||||||||||||||||||||||||||||||||||||||

WHITE SUPREMACIST TOM METZGER WAS ORDERED BY

an Oregon jury to pay $5 million in damages to the family of a black man beaten to death by Metzger's skinheads. Metzger, whose organization is headquartered in Fallbrook, then applied for and received $960 in California welfare payments three days after his assets were seized by the state to help pay the damages.

||||||||||||||||||||||||||||||||||||||||||||||||||||||||||||

A SUNLAND WOMAN DETERMINED TO END IT ALL BY JUMP-

ing from a forty-foot bridge was pulled away from the precipice by a Good Samaritan. In the struggle, the woman fell five feet and was knocked unconscious. The Samaritan grabbed her purse and ran away. "There is no way of telling what his intent was," a police officer said. "He did prevent her from jumping, but whether that was because he was a Good Samaritan or just wanted her purse, we can't tell."

- Percentage of Southern Californians who own guns: 25
- Percentage of Southern Californians who have security systems: 18
- Percentage of Southern Californians who live in a secured dwelling (gate, security fence, or security guard): 16
- Percentage of Southern Californians who have all of the above: 1

THROW AWAY THE PADDLE AND ENTER THE HIGH-TECH

world of corporal punishment. A Montebello physics teacher was placed on administrative leave after he was accused of using a stun gun on three of his ninth-grade students. Not wishing to reject traditional hand tools altogether, however, the teacher held a knife to another kid's throat.

AFTER VOTERS APPROVED PROPOSITION 139, WHICH

would allow inmates to work for private employers, an enterprising fellow requested permission from the Department of Corrections to install a 900 line in the cells of California's most famous inmates. He expected to make his fortune charging callers by the minute to talk with Charles Manson and Sirhan Sirhan. His request was denied, otherwise America would have been subjected to ads like "Call Now! 1-900-ASK-CHARLIE."

WHEN JUDGE HOLLINGSWORTH OF THE TORRANCE SU-

perior Court refused to delay his assault trial, Gregory Ward tried to get even. He refused to put on the 501 Levis and gray sweater his attorney sent for him to wear to court. Asked to appear in his jail blues, the defendant said, "I ain't coming out in nothing." Judge Hollingsworth, a man who tolerates little nonsense, ordered Ward to appear before him dressed or not. Ward chose not, and walked into the courtroom wearing only handcuffs and a shirt the bailiff had tied around Ward's waist.

CHAKA, CALIFORNIA'S MOST PROLIFIC GRAFFITI ARTIST,

was finally arrested after defacing more than $500,000 worth of California property—freeway underpasses, train cars, signposts, buildings, and street lamps. He pleaded no contest to ten counts of vandalism and was ordered to spend 1,560 hours cleaning up his mess. Chaka was also told that he could not "own or possess any spray-paint cans or wide-tip markers." Chaka's future plans: to become an airbrush artist.

IN ONE WEEK IN MAY 1991, THE *HERMOSA BEACH DAILY*

Breeze carried these headlines: WELL-DRESSED MAN ROBS BRINK'S TRUCK and WELL-DRESSED ROBBER ESCAPES AFTER STICK-UP AT BANK OF SAN PEDRO. Apparently two upscale thieves were working the South Bay area. The first man was wearing a dark suit and tie with a white shirt; the other, a gray suit and white shirt, putting a new spin on dressing for success.

FOUR INMATES FROM THE FAIRFIELD PRISON WERE AIDED

by ineptitude in their escape. When one prisoner had trouble making it over a fence, a dispatcher urged him to "try again," thinking the inmate was a teenager trying to sneak into the county parking lot. The jail break wasn't discovered for nearly five hours because the security cameras weren't being watched and fifty-five minutes more passed before dispatchers were notified. Finally, a wrongly entered computer code stretched the getaway time to twelve hours before the California Highway Patrol was notified.

FROM A *HERMOSA BEACH HOMETOWN NEWS* CRIME COL-

umn: "1000 Hermosa Avenue. At approximately 10:30 A.M., a white female was seen putting dirt from a nearby planter into the mail slot of the business. She then placed a pamphlet and a liquid into the slot before doing a 'dance' and running away."

THE WEEK BEFORE NEW YEAR'S EVE IN LOS ANGELES,

ammunition sales are banned. The object is to stop people from firing guns into the air at midnight. In the years preceding the ban, at least one reveler has been killed and dozens injured each New Year.

JAMES LESLIE KARIS, CONVICTED IN THE MURDER OF AN

El Dorado County welfare worker, appealed his conviction to the state Supreme Court because felons were barred from jury duty. The court said that Karis had not proved that the California felon population had "grown so large" that they were necessary to complete a jury.

A REDONDO BEACH MAN WAS CONVICTED OF ASSAULT

with a deadly weapon, sentenced to three years' probation, and fined up to $48,000 after he rammed his model airplane into the side of the Goodyear blimp. The tear in the blimp forced it to land. There were no injuries.

IN TWO DAYS IN 1989, A SAN DIEGO MAN ALLEGEDLY

committed three counts of armed robbery, three counts of armed burglary, two counts of assault with intent to commit rape, one count of attempted robbery, one count of false imprisonment, and one count of assault with force likely to produce great bodily injury. The thirty-year-old man had been released from prison a month earlier with time off for good behavior.

Rodger Fenster is the first person to appear on the TV show "People's Court" to be sentenced to death.

A KU KLUX KLAN LEADER IN LOS ANGELES OBTAINED

county and city fire permits to have a barbecue before he and twenty followers burned a cross in his yard. Permits notwithstanding, he was arrested.

FROM THE "IS THIS LAW REALLY NECESSARY?" DE-
partment:

I California Senate Bill 697 requires the governor to declare December 7 as Pearl Harbor Day each year.

I Senator Bill Lockyer, D-Hayward, pushed through legislation which mandates that state agencies must answer the telephone within ten rings during normal business hours.

I State law now makes it a crime to eat any animal being kept as a house pet.

I Senate Bill 1130 regulates the volume control of California's car sound systems. Music heard more than fifty feet away from a vehicle can result in a traffic citation.

FROM THE *CALIFORNIA REPORTER*:

"*Most simply stated* (the emphasis is mine), appellant on January 29, 1979, was found to be carrying a concealed ice pick of ordinary commercial manufacture when he, among others, was subjected to a precautionary pat down search by officers, who, after observing a traffic violation, had stopped the car in which the detainees were riding. Discovery of the ice pick occasioned the first of the petitions enumerated.

"The second resulted from photographic identification of appellant by the victim as the person who, with numerous others, had participated in relieving one Julian Valdez of the money from his person and in thereafter stealing his car at about 5:30 A.M. on April 28, 1979."

YOU DON'T KNOW MY NAME . . . THE PLUMBER WHO

filmed the brutal beating of Rodney King by the LAPD later realized he'd been had by the media. George Holliday sold his home video to KTLA-TV for $500 only to have it picked up and aired around the world. Holliday, whose attorneys are preparing to sue alleged copyright infringers for $100 million, also appears endorsing a video called "Shoot News and Make Money with Your Camcorder." According to Holliday, "I could have made a lot more money than I did if I knew about the existence of this videotape."

WILLIAM M. BENNETT OF THE STATE BOARD OF EQUILI-

zation was convicted of a misdemeanor for filing false expense reports. When Bennett refused to resign from the Board, Matt Fong, a fellow Board member, began reading this warning to taxpayers who appeared before the tax appeals board. "If you would prefer not having this case decided by a person convicted of fraud against the people of the state of California, then I would be happy to use my board discretion to request such a continuance for you." Bennett is a Democrat; Fong is a Republican.

A NATURAL HISTORY

OF THE SENSELESS

YOU CAN'T FOOL MOTHER NATURE, THEY SAY, BUT NA-
ture is constantly fooling with California. These are not your
run-of-the-mill natural inconveniences like a rained-out picnic,
these are catastrophes of biblical proportions: earthquake, fire,
flood, and pestilence. The rest of the world waits for California
to shear off at its fault lines, but most Californians choose to
ignore the possibility of a quake. After all, with such little
notice, it's impossible to plan a party around one.

In an effort to understand this mass denial, we conducted
a man-on-the street (well, Rodeo Drive, actually) interview with
Jim "Gnarly Dude" Feathers, who, despite his Ohio license
plates, claims to be a California native. When we asked him

what it's like to live on the edge, each morning expecting disaster to hit, he was quick to set us straight.

"A quake is not a disaster," he said. "It is merely a rearrangement of the tectonic plates, a balancing of the universe, sort of like geologic reflexology, you know? Now a disaster, that's like when we found out the Perrier was tainted. It was like worse than water rationing, it was like out there, and we all had to switch to diet sodas. Or a disaster is like when you've got a date with some hot babe and there's a solar flare and your solar-powered hot tub boils over. Or it's like when your personal trainer cancels an appointment and you have to miss a workout, you know? Your muscles get kinked and you feel real bogus and your energy is blocked which throws your aura off and people are like reacting to that.

"Or, it's like when you're driving in your convertible down the Pacific Coast Highway and a pigeon thinks your leather upholstery is a rest stop. Or even worse, it's like when you've had four or five diet sodas and you get stuck on the 405 in rush hour and there's like no bushes on the freeway. I mean they've got those emergency phones and stuff, but you're afraid to leave your car cause it'll be stripped down and sold by the time you get back, and like what are they gonna do anyway, airlift a port-a-potty to you on the freeway?"

Here "Gnarly Dude" paused for breath and we got the hell out of there. You get the picture: earthquake, fire, flood, and pestilence are general phenomena. Californians—the same people who petitioned the Senate to change the state motto to "Me First"—are concerned only with the specific. As in "How does this apply *specifically* to me?" Still, you've got to give them credit: Californians have a remarkable ability to look disaster in the eye . . . and keep on shopping.

||||||||||||||||||||||||||||||||||||||||||||||||||||||||||||

DURING THE RECENT DROUGHT CALIFORNIANS, NOR-

mally a little abnormal, became completely unhinged. A few of their drought-busting ideas:

▌ In order to conserve water, one West L.A. woman dug up her front lawn and had the ground covered with green concrete. A Beverly Hills resident put his Porsche on blocks in his front yard so that he could wash his car and water his lawn at the same time.

▌ The Water Education Foundation in Sacramento received a suggestion that officials run candlewicks from the ocean to California homes. The wicks would absorb the salt and provide fresh drinking water—one drop at a time.

▌ Another do-gooder suggested that men be prohibited from shaving until the drought ended.

▌ Everyone jumped on the conservation bandwagon: a car wash in Arcadia gave away bricks to its customers, telling them to place them in their toilet tanks to cut down on water usage. Not a good idea, the Department of Water and Power later said. Bricks break down in water, gumming up the works.

▌ An L.A. man suggested that water usage could be significantly reduced if Californians would use the sink to relieve themselves rather than the toilet.

▌ A volleyball-film producer wanted to tow massive icebergs from Antarctica to California to provide fresh water. The California legislature took the idea seriously enough to pass a resolution which urged federal agencies to "support a pilot program . . . promising a water supply from imported Antarctic icebergs for California."

An engineer labored for years over plans for a solar greenhouse that would pump enough salt-water steam into the atmosphere to create rain clouds. The greenhouse would be 6.7 miles in diameter, use sixteen thousand acres of glass, and cost over $30 billion. Expected rainfall: one inch per day.

In 1991, the California Senate passed a bill mandating water meters on all new homes in California. The bill does not say, however, that the meters must work.

L.A. Times headline: RATIONING MEAT WILL SAVE WATER, VEGETARIANS SAY.

AS THE DROUGHT BEGAN TO EASE IN 1991, CALIFORNIANS

were asked to keep their water consumption under three hundred gallons a day. Governor Pete Wilson used 650 gallons a day during the month of June, tripling his water usage from previous months.

IN MONTECITO, WHERE THE WATER SHORTAGE WAS

critical, billionaire Harold Simmons blithely ignored mandatory rationing, using enough water, officials said, to take care of a family of four for twenty-eight years. A twenty-five-thousand-dollar fine didn't faze Simmons, nor did restricting the flow of water to his twenty-three-acre estate. Simmons simply had truckloads of fresh water shipped in.

"HONEY, DO WE KNOW THE SCHLEGELS
WELL ENOUGH NOT TO FLUSH?"

▌ First, the good news: California's first desalination plant on Catalina Island is processing sea water into drinking water.

▌ Now, the bad news: The processed water smells and tastes like rotten eggs.

A COUNTY GEOLOGIST NEAR SAN FRANCISCO ACCURATELY

predicted the 1989 Loma Prieta earthquake by counting the number of lost cats and dogs in the classifieds. When he counted twenty-seven missing cats and fifty-seven lost dogs, he knew a big one was on the way.

IS THERE A CLIO AWARD FOR BAD TASTE? FIVE SAN FRAN-

cisco ad agencies put together an exhibition less than a year after the devastating Loma Prieta quake. The front of their invitation read: "See the kind of work you do when every ad could be your last." Inside was a photo of the mangled Nimitz freeway, which collapsed during the earthquake.

WHEN THE 1987 WHITTIER EARTHQUAKE BEGAN SHAK-

ing the newsroom, a terrified KNBC anchorman dove under his desk *while he was on the air*.

IN OCTOBER 1991, INDIO, NEAR THE SAN ANDREAS FAULT,

experienced 117 small earthquakes. Seven of the tremors measured 3.0 or greater on the Richter scale. Scientists, however, kept their sense of humor. The earthquakes commenced about the time that televangelist Jimmy Swaggart was stopped by Indio police and found to be in a compromising position with his passenger, who was a prostitute. In his honor, the scientists named the series of temblors the "Jimmy Swaggart Swarm."

SUPERVISORS AT A CALIFORNIA ADMINISTRATIVE AGENCY

have red phones for emergencies. During the Sierra Madre earthquake in June 1991, they picked up their phones to receive further instructions. A taped message told them: "We're all doomed. Drop your pants and kiss your ass goodbye."

THE CALIFORNIA SENATE HAS DECLARED THE OFFICIAL

state nickname, motto, colors, animal, bird, fish, flower, fossil, gem, insect, marine mammal, mineral, reptile, song, stone, and tree. In 1991, the Senate got down to business and designated an eight-thousand-year-old chipped stone resembling a bear as the official state artifact.

A STUDY PRESENTED IN SAN DIEGO REPORTED THAT DI-

nosaur flatulence may have contributed to global warming some seventy-five million years ago. Methane gas emitted as part of the dinosaurs' digestive process created a kind of greenhouse effect, the scientists said, which supports the current theory that the methane gas being expelled by cows is contributing to modern-day global warming.

IN THE SPRING OF 1990, OVER THREE HUNDRED SEA LIONS

hauled themselves out of the water and took up residence on a dock near Fisherman's Wharf in San Francisco. At first, the seven-hundred-pound marine mammals were a delight and a tourist attraction, but the situation soon turned ugly. The sea lions used the dock as their toilet, wreaked havoc on the pier, and chased seagoers away from their boats. Sheila Candor, manager of the marina, said, "We didn't know if you let them get a flipper in the door, there's no stopping them. They keep everyone awake with their personal habits and their partying, and they smell bad. They're like the guests from hell."

MALIBU HAS DECLARED ITSELF AN OFFICIAL DOLPHIN

sanctuary and considers the marine mammals citizens.

C'MON MIKE, WOULD THE DOLPHINS GIVE UP THEIR FAVORITE SANDWICH TO SAVE OUR BUTTS?

"ZEKE THE SHEIK" FROM ALTADENA MAINTAINS A THIRTY-

foot-high, two-hundred-foot-wide compost heap in his back-yard. He has tended the collection of mulch, household scraps, and manure for more than seventeen years, proclaiming that compost is his life's work and "the key of energy that will eventually set mankind free from misery and gravity." Altadena authorities do not look fondly upon the project, however. The heap is a breeding ground for flies and has a tendency to spontaneously combust.

A SOUTHERN CALIFORNIA CHEMICAL COMPANY SPONSORS

an annual contest called "The Great American Roach-Off." Entrants who submit the largest roaches win thousands of dollars. Contest rules state that roaches must be dead and "unaltered," which means they cannot be "stretched, squished, or smashed."

TWICE DURING THE SUMMER OF 1990, THE ROWENA RES-

ervoir in Los Feliz was shut down. It seems that the midge fly larvae population, aided by high summer temperatures, got out of control. When residents turned on their faucets, the white larvae poured out of their taps.

AFTER MUCH DEBATE, AFRICAN GOLIATH FROGS, A PAR-

ticularly large breed of amphibians, were allowed to participate in the Calaveras County Frog Jumping Contest. Officials ruled that the Goliaths must leap from the same regulation pads that have been used in the past. "As long as they can fit their feet on the pad, they can compete," one member of the board of directors said. "Those are the rules and any frog who obeys the rules should be able to compete."

CHERRY VALLEY WAS SWARMED WITH FLIES. ONE

woman killed a hundred on her screened porch one morning, and the building facades, covered with flies, looked black. Residents pointed to the local chicken ranches as the source, but a county health official had a different explanation. "Many times these flies will grow from leftover clippings in people's lawnmowers."

IN THE FIRST OPERATION OF ITS KIND, A SEVEN-YEAR-

old kangaroo from the San Francisco zoo received a pacemaker. The surgery was performed by a team of cardiologists from the University of California Medical School.

THE *LOS ANGELES TIMES* CARRIED A NOTICE STATING

that the Natural History Museum would conduct the Dick Davenport Memorial Bird Walk at the Rose Garden in Exposition Park. The notice went on to say that Davenport died while photographing a Bachman's warbler in Yosemite National Park. The announcement was printed with all seriousness and respect. The paper did not realize that Dick Davenport was a character from the comic strip "Doonesbury."

FROM THE "WE COULD HAVE TOLD YOU THAT" FILE: EV-

olutionary biologists at the University of California at Irvine conducted a study on snake locomotion. Outfitted with miniature oxygen masks, snakes were forced to crawl on treadmills while the scientists observed and took notes. Conclusions? "Without legs, snakes—because of their cylindrical shape—can squeeze through very small openings."

HANNIBAL, A SIXTEEN-YEAR-OLD ELEPHANT, NEEDED A

pedicure—a procedure that requires sedation. When Hannibal failed to respond to the tranquilizer antidote, the fire department was called in. In order to rouse the elephant, firemen used their tow truck to haul Hannibal to his feet (being careful, we're sure, not to mess up the nail job).

REELING FROM AN ONSLAUGHT OF YELLOW JACKETS IN

which as many as thirty people were stung in one week, the Los Angeles Zoo was forced to erect a sign warning visitors to "Bee Aware" that yellow jackets are drawn to sweet syrupy drinks. "They can find a Slurpee at 10,000 paces," said interim zoo director Jerry Greenwalt.

OVER ONE HUNDRED AND FIFTY WILD PEACOCKS HAVE

taken over Rolling Hills Estates in Palos Verdes. Residents of the exclusive community are awakened each morning at 4 A.M. by the ghostly screams of the fowl. Citizens are further inconvenienced by the pack-traveling birds, which destroy lawns, eat flowers, and leave their droppings poolside. Desperate to keep the peace, the city council called in a peafowl farmer from Iowa who, for $200 a day plus expenses, will advise residents on ways to cope with the peacocks. Residents are also hopeful that he will be able to lure the birds away from their community.

PARK RANGERS AT YOSEMITE NATIONAL PARK ARE

trying to convince tourists that the park's deer are not like Bambi; they are downright dangerous. Trusting deer-lovers who come too close have been gored by Yosemite deer. One tourist, ignoring the warnings, tried to climb on a deer's back to ride it. Luckily, the deer merely ran away instead of skewering him.

||||||||||||||||||||||||||||||||||||||||||||||||||||||||

THE DEVIL'S PUNCHBOWL, A CALIFORNIA PARK, GIVES

nature lovers a firsthand look at rattlesnakes, red wasps called cowkillers, and a warning: "Area contains rodents whose fleas may carry bubonic plague—enter at own risk." I think not.

ON THE BEACH

YOU'VE SEEN ALL OF THOSE BEER ADS FILMED ON THE beaches of Southern California. You've seen those perfect-ten bodies, the thong bikinis, the bronzed Greek gods. You've told yourself, "Nobody really looks like that. Those are the same six models who have nothing better to do than exercise all day." Let me debunk a myth for you. Those are not models, they are real people, and everyone who goes to the beach in California looks like that. Quite simply, if you do not look like that, they will not let you on the beach.

Let us pause a moment while your illusions shatter. (Don't forget to pick up the shards, they'll cut your feet.) It's your fault, really—if you had given some thought to the beach situation, the reality would have dawned on you. You know how you feel when you visit East and Gulf Coast beaches and you're a little uncomfortable because you're pale and lumpy. Then you see a bus unloading a lot of men and women who look like Moby Dick's first cousins: really, really huge and so white they look like they've been grown in a mushroom culture. And you feel better about yourself because the men's stomachs hang over their baggy swim trunks and the women all have those bathing suits with the little skirts on 'em to cover their chafed thighs. Where do you think they found these folks? Correct, California. They were rounded up and put in a detention camp near Barstow and bussed to Vero Beach.

Now, let me debunk your other myth. "I could look like those California tens if I lost (*fill in the number here*) pounds and joined a health spa." Forget it. You will never look like that, not if you lost twice that amount and spent eighteen hours a day, every day, for the rest of your natural life on a Stairmaster. It just ain't gonna happen. Why? Let's go back to the moment of your conception. Did your mother look like Yvette Mimieux? Was your father often mistaken for Tab Hunter? The five of you who said "yes" may keep reading, the rest of you, don't waste your time.

Let's weed out those remaining five: *If* your parents looked like the aforementioned, did you begin a rigorous exercise program *before* the doctor slapped you? Did you prefer wheat germ to strained pears? Were your first words "flexor digitorum profundus"? Do you have any idea what I am talking about?

If you have answered "no" to any of these questions, you may not set even one toe on a California beach. If you have answered "yes" to any of these questions, you are either a pathological liar or you are reading this book at Zuma.

By now, if you have any curiosity at all, you are asking yourself, "How does she know so much about California beaches? Is she Ms. Perfect Body 1993?" No, not exactly. You see, they have these lifeguard stations at the beach, they're kind of square and squatty and painted with black and white stripes, and I have this black and white bathing suit, see, and if you move really, really slowly . . .

‖‖‖

AFTER THE LOUISIANA-PACIFIC CORPORATION AND SIMP-

son Paper Company committed more than forty thousand violations of the Clean Water Act, Surfriders, a political action group comprised of fifteen thousand surfers, took the mega-corporations to court and won. In addition to a $5.8 million fine, the two companies have been told they must build solar-powered showers so that surfers can rinse off toxic residue picked up in the still-contaminated waters.

‖‖‖

AT HUNTINGTON BEACH, BIKE RIDERS ARE HELD TO A

five-mile-per-hour speed limit when pedestrians are around. Bike speeding got so out of control during the summer of 1991 that police were called in to enforce the law. They did —using hand-held radar guns to catch the offenders.

ACCORDING TO LEGEND, SURFING BEGAN IN CALIFORNIA

over one hundred years ago when two Hawaiian princes introduced the sport at Santa Cruz. It is documented, however, that Duke Kahanamoku helped draw attention to surfing by giving exhibits at Santa Cruz in 1912.

IN AUGUST 1989, ON A CALM DAY, THE SEA OFF MALIBU

began to swell and surge. Ten-foot waves crashed down on unsuspecting swimmers. One man was killed and rescuers pulled seventy people from the ocean. Two of those rescued had to be hospitalized. Surfers in the Malibu Classic Surfing Competition, however, had a personal philosophy that helped them through the crisis. According to a member of the Professional Surfing Association, the sight of the huge waves left competitors and officials "stoked beyond belief."

WHEN HUNDREDS OF BABY JUMBO SQUID—SOME OF

them three feet long—began washing ashore at San Onofre and San Diego, the lifeguards weren't dismayed. They saw the squid-filled beaches as a huge seafood buffet. Lifeguard Shaun Healy said, "We've got sixty pounds of ice on the way and we're going to cut these guys up and stash them away. Then we'll have a giant cookout on the beach."

LINDA BROWER WATCHES A HOLE FOR A LIVING. THE U.S.

Army Corps of Engineers pays her $8.50 an hour to watch a twenty-foot-wide, six-foot-deep hole at Oceanside Beach to make sure swimmers stay away. The hole was created by a sand distribution project that takes sand from the city marina, runs it through a pipeline, and redistributes it along the coast. Before she was a hole-watcher, Brower spent fifteen years cutting stencils for bowling shirt letters.

CHAD BEATTY OF REDONDO BEACH AND SEVEN FRIENDS

decided to surf the Java coastline. Their plans went awry, however, and the eight men and four Indonesian crewmen were adrift in the Indian Ocean for ten days. Beatty's take on the ordeal: "I think we missed the good surf."

CONVERSATION BETWEEN TWO NURSES OVERHEARD IN

a doctor's office:
    "What did you write down on her chart?"
    "Allergy to wetsuit material."
    "What does she do?"
    "Works in a surf shop."
    "Too bad."

IN 1983, ATTENDANCE AT L.A. COUNTY BEACHES HIT AN

all-time high of seventy million. Since then people have been staying away in droves. By 1990, annual attendance had dropped to fifty-six million. Most frequently cited reasons for staying away: water pollution and fear of sun.

ACCORDING TO *SURFER* MAGAZINE EDITOR STEVE HAWK,

"Oregon surfers sometimes defecate on cars that have California license plates."

A SURF SHOP OWNER WAS ARRESTED ON DRUG CHARGES

and his shop closed. Sometime later, a hand-lettered sign was seen on the building: CLOSED DUE TO SNOW.

THINGS SURFERS DO TO ATTRACT GOOD WAVES:

burn surfboards
stop shaving
pray

- drive a VW bug, preferably pre-1967
- bite off tops of floating kelp bulbs
- bark like seals

EMPLOYEES AT A MALIBU BRANCH BANK WEAR SWIM-
suits under their clothes so they can hit the beach at lunch time.

RICHARD LYMAN OF REDONDO BEACH WAS RIDING HIS
bike along the bike path when a skater in front of him collapsed. Fortunately, Lyman kept a cellular phone attached to his bike. Paramedics were summoned immediately and the skater, who had suffered a heart attack, survived. "I sell cellular phones," Lyman said, "and I always tell people that they can be lifesavers in an emergency."

HOPPY SWARTS, FOUNDER OF THE U.S. SURFING ASSO-
ciation, caught his first wave at Hermosa Beach in 1934. Although he was an electrical engineer who had worked at MIT during World War II, Hoppy's first love was surfing. When he died in 1988 at 71, his friends and family gathered at Redondo

Beach to send him on his way. Hoppy's ashes were carried on his grandson's surfboard for a final ride, then they were scattered among the waves.

ACCORDING TO JON SHEINBERG, A MOTION PICTURE EX-
ecutive, Beverly Hills High School offered surfing classes in the sixties.

THERE'S AN OLD, WORN-OUT JOKE ABOUT BUYING BEACH-
front property in Arizona after the BIG ONE hits California. Two Arizona disc jockeys took the joke seriously and organized an event they hoped would speed up the process. Glenn Beck and Tim Hattrick of KOY-FM sent four men, each weighing over 250 pounds, to California. On the day Nostradamus predicted that Los Angeles would fall into the sea, the four men assembled at Venice Beach to perform jumping jacks. The organizers hoped the jolt to the tectonic plates would precipitate an earthquake.

▌▌

OVERHEARD IN A HERMOSA BEACH BAR IN REFERENCE TO

a middle-aged, obviously inebriated patron: "Look at him. In the sixties he was one of the world's best surfers. Used to be he could walk on water. Now he can't even walk across the parking lot."

▌▌

THE FIRST COMPANY TO TAKE ADVANTAGE OF PACIFIC

Bell's new 1-900 service was Surfline, Inc. For anywhere from 85 cents to $2, callers can receive information about surf conditions. (In California, there is a local number.) Surfline receives over one million calls a year. A glossary is needed, however, to decipher the descriptions: waves can be backwashy, mushin' out, or backin' off. The water can have workable shoulders, pipes, stables, or scattered peaks. Best to remember that "glassy" means good conditions and "blown out" means don't bother.

▌▌

WHEN A SEWAGE LINE RUPTURED OFF THE COAST OF SAN

Diego in 1992, 180 million gallons of sewage poured into the ocean each day for a week. One hundred miles of coastline were closed and health department officials warned that contact with the bacteria-infested surf could result in dysentery, hepatitis, and typhoid. Surfers, however, were undaunted and took to the waves as usual. One surfer reasoned, "I live to surf. If I'm going to die or get sick, I'd rather have it happen in the ocean. If the water is green and glowing, I'll still go out. Maybe I'll get some cancer bump on my head and they'll say it's the result of surfing. Who knows?"

‖‖

FATHER BRUCE OSBORN, PASTOR OF OUR LADY OF GUAD-

alupe Church in L.A., carries a surfboard in his Jeep, wears cutoffs and T-shirts when he's off duty, and surfs whenever he can find the time. His parishioners call him "Father Rad."

‖‖

BECAUSE LIFEGUARDS SPEND INORDINATE AMOUNTS OF

time in the sun and because they are forced to go into toxic waters even when the beaches are closed for health reasons, State Senator Art Torres (D-Los Angeles) sponsored a bill that would give lifeguards the same cancer benefits afforded to California police and firefighters. If passed, the bill would force city and county governments to prove that the cancer was *not* caused by the sun or toxic runoff. Opponents of the bill said the law would make it a "slam dunk" for the lifeguards.

||||||||||||||||||||||||||||||||||||||||||||||||||||||||||||||||||

LAGUNA BEACH GAVE THE GO-AHEAD TO ARTIST WYLAND

to paint a 116,000-square-foot mural—the world's largest whale mural—on the walls of the Laguna Beach Arena. An anonymous critic, trying to derail the project, sent town officials copies of a 1981 issue of *Cheri*, a sexually explicit magazine, featuring a photo layout of Wyland with a nude model. Wyland dismissed the ensuing controversy, saying, "Michelangelo painted nudes too." (Yeah, but did he use an airbrush?)

||||||||||||||||||||||||||||||||||||||||||||||||||||||||||||||||||

BUOYED BY THEIR FIRST SUCCESS, THE SURFRIDER FOUN-

dation took on Chevron Oil Corporation for building something called a "rock groin" to protect underground pipes in Santa Monica Bay. The rock groin changed the wave patterns off El Segundo, eliminating the wide tubes the surfers love. Now the waves are shallow and dangerous—"911 waves," the surfers call them, because they can destroy a surfboard and surfer when they break on the beach. Surfriders, with the California Coastal Commission on its side, wanted Chevron to build sandbars that would restore the wide tubes. Chevron countered with an offer to build an on-beach shower for the surfers, but the answer was "No way." The least the surfers will settle for is $250,000 to research artificial reefs.

IN ORDER TO CREATE A FIREBREAK DURING THE DROUGHT

of 1991, Laguna Beach firefighters used five hundred goats to eat brush, weeds, and wild oats growing near lavish beach homes. Four goatherds and three collies were needed to keep the goats in line and on the job.

FOLLOWING THE FOUR-HUNDRED-THOUSAND-GALLON

American Trader oil spill, Huntington Beach was closed. But the waves breaking off the pier beckoned and twenty-two-year-old surfer Todd Bonnet took to the sea. He was arrested shortly thereafter. Bonnet didn't see what the big deal was, saying, "I surfed in sewage last month." What would it take to keep him out of the water? "Maybe nuclear waste."

COMPETITION FOR WAVES HAS GROWN SO FIERCE, CAL-

ifornia surfers have started surfing at night. One surfer claimed that at 1:00 A.M. fourteen other surfers were jostling him for waves.

POINT DUME IN MALIBU IS SO EXCLUSIVE THAT SURFERS
must have a key to enter the beach.

AN APOCRYPHAL TALE, PERHAPS, BUT IT HAS BECOME
part of surf lore: Otis Chandler, former head of the *Los Angeles Times*, was an avid surfer whose favorite spot was called Killer Dana. It is said that stuffy business meetings with Chandler's associates were often interrupted by a butler bearing a message on a silver tray. Chandler would read the message, excuse himself, and make a quick exit. One staffer, overcome by curiosity, picked up the note Chandler had left behind. It said: "Surf's up."

BUMPER STICKER: GOD CREATED SURFBOARDS SO THAT
THE TRULY GIFTED WOULDN'T RULE THE WORLD.

(UN)REAL ESTATE

THE EVENT WAS UNPRECEDENTED IN THE ANNALS OF
Beverly Hills real estate. An agency so exclusive it refused to
accept clients decided (actually the bankruptcy judge ordered
it) to hold an open house. For those of you who do not understand, Beverly Hills real estate agents are repelled by the
idea of holding an open house because they must then deal
with "real" people (those without fame and money) or, as they
like to call us, "the scum of the earth."

I am not daunted by their condescension. (I am rarely
daunted. "Fools rush in," they say and I am following close
on their heels.) An open house is a good way to kill a Sunday
afternoon. So I put on my blue jeans, my white T-shirt, my

blue blazer—the uniform of the rich for whom I hoped to be mistaken—and joined the tour.

Our guide was a lovely twentysomething, a woman who seemed to exude wealth and privilege. It was obvious her skin had never known the touch of synthetic fabrics or drugstore makeup.

"Gather round," she said. "Before entering, I would like to tell you about the house. It was built in the 1920s by a cocoa butter magnate who produced silent films. Rather small by today's standards, the original house had six thousand square feet. Our client, an actress whose name we are not at liberty to reveal (but whose likeness in the form of 8 × 10 glossies was plastered throughout the house) made a few changes after the birth of her third love child. You can expect to spend a better part of the next month on this tour. Can you commit?" Stupidly, like sheep to the slaughter, we nodded our heads "yes." Ms. Twentysomething smiled and said, "Let's proceed."

We proceeded and proceeded and proceeded, through fifty-three bathrooms, seventy-six bedrooms, a bowling alley, a theater, six kitchens, and a replica of Versailles built to scale off the master bedroom.

By now it was Tuesday. We had not eaten since early the previous day when we ordered takeout from the authentically reproduced Howard Johnson's, which the actress had added because love child number two likes fried clams and orange sherbet.

This tour had become a real people's endurance test. Our guide, however, seemed to be thriving. Like most Beverly Hills women and some exotic plants, she existed, for the most part, on air. The rest of her sustenance she drew from her silk blouse. This girl had been trained from birth to walk in four-inch heels; her skirt did not wrinkle, her hair did not move. We, however, looked as if we had just fought the battle of the Alamo armed only with our clothes.

At this point I welcomed the firing squad. But no, there were several acres of house left. An untold number of bidets to demonstrate, endless closet space to explore, and, of course, who wanted to miss the full-scale replica of the Pentagon that adjoined the rec room?

Finally, somewhere between St. Peter's Basilica and the Leaning Tower of Pisa, which had been moved from Europe and installed in the new wing, our guide stopped.

"For those of you who do not wish to continue the tour, you may leave us here. But first, are there any questions?"

I raised my hand weakly. "Why," I asked, "did she put this house on the market? It's so lovely."

Ms. Twentysomething eyed me with disdain (although I'm sure she couldn't spell it).

"Don't you people read the papers?" she huffed. "Our client is having another baby."

I stared at her blankly. Confused by hunger and exhaustion, I couldn't grasp what she was saying.

"A baby," she repeated and gave me a look that said, "No wonder you people live in duplexes."

She huffed once more and explained slowly, "Our client can't possibly raise four children in this house. There simply isn't enough room."

I left the tour baffled. Where could this woman possibly find a larger home? I got my answer a few days later: Our actress, a Hollywood insider reported, has just bought the Vatican.

LITTLE GARY JACOBS IS A BOY. BOYS LIKE TO BUILD FORTS

in the backyard. After Gary and his friends put together a rough-and-tumble plywood treehouse in the Jacobses' yard, they were ordered to tear it down by the Westlake Island Property Association, which said it was not in keeping with aesthetic standards. An architect took pity on the kids and drew up plans for a more tasteful split-level. The kids were then required to present the building project to the architectural committee of the association just as any contractor would. According to the association chairwoman, "No one is trying to beat up these kids. But if you're going to teach them, teach them properly."

ACCORDING TO A *SAN DIEGO UNION* HEADLINE, HORTON

PLAZA'S UGLY BEHIND IS GETTING A FACE-LIFT. The article goes on to quote city architect Mike Stepner, who said, "Horton Plaza for the last several years has been mooning the Gaslamp quarter."

WHEN A FIFTY-YEAR-OLD SEWER PIPE NEEDED RENO-

vation in Laguna Beach, TV cables and sewers were taken out of service for a month. Residents were told not to run water for bathing, cooking, cleaning, or flushing from 9:00 A.M. until midnight. In order to make the situation more bearable, portable toilets were installed. Somehow it is hard to picture one Victoria Beach resident, the Divine Miss M, finding these conditions tolerable. Another resident inconvenienced by the construction said, "No cable and no toilet. It's hell in this neighborhood."

GARY LEONARD SPENT SIX YEARS COLLECTING TRASH, OR

should we say *material*, for the huge sculpture that sat in the front yard of his Echo Park home. Made up of unwanted household items, rusted auto parts, and garden implements, the work of art became the center of controversy when Leonard was forced to sell his home. The investor who bought the house did not share Leonard's aesthetic tastes; he wanted the thing destroyed. In an effort to preserve his work, Leonard tried to have the sculpture declared a landmark, but the Cultural Heritage Commission turned him down. According to the investor, the Commission had made a wise decision. "Sure, it's an interesting thing," he said. "But you could take the position that the city dump is art."

WITH THE TRADE-IN OF THEIR OLD HOUSE AND $4 MIL-

lion wired by daddy, four college boys from Djakarta purchased a home in Beverly Hills that had been listed for $7.35 million. The twelve-thousand-square-foot house has five bedrooms, maid's quarters, a tennis court, and a swimming pool. The only drawback: there isn't enough parking space for the boys' Rolls-Royce, Ferrari, two BMWs, and Mercedes-Benz.

ACCORDING TO THE U.S. DEPARTMENT OF HOUSING AND

Urban Development, in 1989 Beverly Hills was deemed to be one of the cities that needed housing renovation subsidies most.

GRAB YOUR BUCKETS. WHEN RANCHO LA BREA, SITE OF

the famous tar pits, was deeded to Jose Roche and Jose Antonio Carrillo, it was granted with the proviso that residents of the pueblo, now known as Los Angeles, could forever use tar from the pit to seal their roofs and ships.

WESTLAKE VILLAGE, WHICH SEEMS TO HAVE MORE THAN

its share of difficulties, has been defiled again. The owners of the Westlake Sporthouse wanted to paint the building's exterior gray. According to the city ordinance, however, all buildings must be painted earth tones. Sporthouse owners argued that gray, a predominant color in nature, is an earth tone. A meeting was called and, after some debate, the City Council determined that neither gray nor green were earth tones. To prevent further misunderstanding, the ordinance was revised to say that only "subdued shades of brown, tan, beige, and off-white" are earth tones. According to Westlake Village Planning Director Robert Theobald, "While it can certainly be argued that gray is an earth tone—rocks are gray—that does not reflect the traditional character of Westlake Village."

‖‖‖

A JAPANESE SURGEON BOUGHT RONALD REAGAN'S FOR-mer home, had it demolished, and in its stead built a ten-bath, five-dome Moroccan palace with two reflecting pools on the lawn. The contractor now uses a marble slab, part of Reagan's old shower, as his desk.

‖‖‖

AT THE "DIVINE DESIGN AND FANTASY AUCTION" IN L.A.,one bidder paid $110,000 to have artist David Hockney paint the bottom of his swimming pool. (A dinner at the White House went for a mere $5,500.)

‖‖‖

SPEAKING OF DIVINE DESIGN, THE BRADBURY BUILDING,built in 1893 in Los Angeles, was designed by George H. Wyman, who was a sci-fi buff. Wyman used a Ouija board to contact

The Bradbury Building, Los Angeles. Its designer was said to consult a Ouija Board. (SECURITY
PACIFIC COLLECTION/LOS ANGELES PUBLIC LIBRARY)

his dead brother, who told him to take the job. Wyman's design
inspiration was a science fiction novel that described the model
building of the 21st century. Fittingly, the Bradbury Building
was prominently featured in the cyberpunk film *Blade Runner*.

‖‖

THE PASADENA BUBBLE HOUSE, BUILT IN 1946, WAS CON-

structed by pouring concrete over a mesh-covered inflated
balloon. The Bubble House was then touted as an example of
affordable housing with a construction cost of $10,000. 1991
asking price: $500,000.

||||||||||||||||||||||||||||||||||||||||||||||||||||||||||

LASSIE NEEDED NEW DIGS, SO A BEVERLY HILLS INTERIOR

design firm was called in to do the job. Their plans resulted in a two-story doghouse complete with murals, antique bookcases, and photos of Rin Tin Tin and Flipper.

||||||||||||||||||||||||||||||||||||||||||||||||||||||||||

AN ENTERPRISING BEVERLY HILLS REAL ESTATE AGENT

had his business cards laminated so that he could pass them out around hotel swimming pools.

||||||||||||||||||||||||||||||||||||||||||||||||||||||||||

DAVID GEFFEN, RECORD MOGUL (HIS CONTRACT STIPU-

lates that his name shall always be preceded or followed by this title which we understand has nothing to do with skiing and everything to do with Hollywood people sucking up to him), needed a little place in town, so he plunked down $3 million for a *pied-à-terre* (French for "excess so wretched it is unspeakable in English or any other Germanic language"). His "temporary housing" comes with a pool, an ocean view, and a "knoll"—not to be confused with a mogul. Now David won't have to make that long and arduous trip to his $47.5 million, nine-acre Beverly Hills estate.

MADELLINE GALLAY CHOSE HER HOLLYWOOD HOME BE-

cause it was "vulgarly strong." The house is surrounded by a fortress wall embedded with shards of broken glass.

SAN FERNANDO VALLEY RESIDENTS FORCED TO SHARE A

ZIP Code with Sepulveda, a community they deemed beneath them, asked the Postmaster General to grant them a separate ZIP Code. Sepulveda, they whined, was seedy, it had prostitutes and drug dealers, and somehow, they reasoned, sharing the same ZIP Code would reflect badly on their tonier neighborhoods. The U.S. Postal Service turned down the request, saying, "We wouldn't provide another ZIP Code just to provide an identity difference. They're too precious to hand out just like that."

CHARLIE CHAPLIN WAS SO TIGHTFISTED HE ENLISTED SET

carpenters to build his fourteen-room Beverly Hills home. When the house began to fall apart a few years later, it became known as the "Breakaway House."

A SEVENTY-FOOT-TALL BOUGAINVILLEA VINE IN GLEN-
dora has been declared a state historical landmark.

WHEN BABY MADE THREE FOR ACTRESS ANN JILLIAN
and her husband, their 5,200-square-foot home suddenly felt cramped. In order to accommodate the newcomer, Ms. Jillian spent $500,000 renovating the house. The renovation project included a custom-built closet for baby's gifts, an intercom and video surveillance system to monitor the baby's crib, a "sexy shower for a fat guy" (Ms. Jillian's husband), and an art gallery. "If you can't spend money on your home," Ms. Jillian said, "you can't spend it anywhere."

AFTER TWENTY YEARS AS A SINGER, DORIS KING GOT
into the real estate business. She now calls herself "The Singing Realtor" and will belt out a song—usually her version of "Love For Sale," in which she substitutes "house" for "love"—at the drop of a client's business card. "In today's market," King said, "you have to be different. These are million-dollar properties."

ONE L.A. BUSINESSMAN SPENT $400,000 FOR A SOLID

bronze and walnut staircase *railing* for his home.

OOPS. LOU SCHEIBER OF TORRANCE WANTED ONLY TO

improve his ocean view, so he got a permit to move fifty cubic yards of dirt from his lot. The bulldozer operator got a little carried away, moving 970 cubic yards of earth, virtually eliminating the bluff Scheiber's house sits on. In an effort to correct the damage, Scheiber asked permission from the California Coastal Commission to buttress the sagging slope. The Commission turned him down, saying that they would never have given him permission to remove that much dirt in the first place.

BOB McJONES HAS A SLIPPAGE PROBLEM OF ANOTHER

sort. The site of his Rancho Palos Verdes home is part of the Portuguese Bend landslide, a tract of land that has been shifting and slipping for over thirty years. Since McJones bought the place for $10,000 in 1975, the site has dropped another five feet. Not to worry. McJones set his house on three massive shipping containers that can be raised or lowered to keep the house level. "It's no harder," he said, "than changing a tire on your car."

MICHAEL AND KAREN GRAHAM, JUST MARRIED, BOUGHT

their San Jose dream home from a retired nurse. Wanting to spruce up the place, the couple tried to plant a tree and found that their yard was full of medical waste. Authorities examined the site and estimated that the cleanup would cost $1 million and that the Grahams were liable. Later the couple found out that for years the retired nurse had been bringing home used syringes, dialysis bags, feeding tubes, and other medical waste from the nursing home where she worked. When asked why, the woman explained that she had buried the stuff in her yard and in the creekbed to frighten away gophers and other rodents.

WHEN CARMEN AND LOU WARSHAW NEEDED A NEW

roof on their Beverly Hills home, they were a tad particular about who did the job. The Warshaws imported six artisans from Shanghai, put them up in condos, and hired an interpreter to work with the men. Three hundred thousand handcrafted tiles and six months later, the job was complete.

IN 1921, SIMON RODIA BEGAN SCAVENGING L.A. FOR BITS

of junk. For the next thirty-three years he built towers from iron, tin, green glass bottles, broken tiles, and over seventy

Simon Rodia used over 70,000 seashells in the construction of the Watts Towers. (SECURITY PACIFIC COLLECTION/LOS ANGELES PUBLIC LIBRARY)

thousand seashells. Two of the towers reached one hundred feet in height. After Rodia left Los Angeles in 1954, the Watts Towers were threatened with demolition. Public support saved them, however, and today Rodia's towers are owned and protected by the state.

AFTER HER MOTHER DIED, FRANCINE KATZENBOGEN TOOK

over the care of mom's twenty cats. Problems started when neighbors learned about Francine's plan to move the cats into the $100,000 guest house she had built for them at her Laurel Canyon estate. The 1200-square-foot building had six rooms painted dove gray with gray tile floors. It was equipped with scratching posts, "lounging platforms," and skylights "so the cats wouldn't get bored." One neighbor took particular offense to the cat's-eye-level windows, saying that the thought of having twenty pairs of eyes staring at her gave her "the willies." Another neighbor felt that if they allowed twenty cats, the neighborhood would soon be overrun by those potbellied Vietnamese pigs. Go figure.

GORDON AND MARY AUGHINBAUGH'S PALOS VERDES

house was a dream—6,000 square feet styled like an eighteenth-century French country house, ocean views, and a private chapel. The house, with its twenty-inch-thick walls, was built to last. That is, until the Palos Verdes Homeowners Association got irked because the Aughinbaughs had spent fourteen years on the house and it still wasn't finished. The Association rules stated that one must "proceed diligently" when building a home in Palos Verdes, so the Association went to court and got an order to have the house demolished. There is still hope for the Aughinbaughs' $1 million investment. The first contractor called to price the demolition job refused to get involved.

WHEN DAVID HOCKNEY PAINTED THE BOTTOM OF THE

Hollywood Roosevelt Hotel's swimming pool, officials said the painting, which looks like a swarm of parentheses, might confuse the lifeguards. All is well, however; the ever-vigilant California Legislature passed a bill that said the artwork was not a hazard.

‖‖

EVERYONE WAS EXCITED WHEN JOSHUA A. PERPER OF

Pittsburgh agreed to serve as the L.A. county coroner—until Mrs. Perper came to Los Angeles to look for a house. Her pronouncement: "In California, everything looks like a slum." The Perpers stayed in Pittsburgh.

‖‖

L.A. DEVELOPER ALEXANDER COLER'S THIRTY-SEVEN-

thousand-square-foot house has one hundred rooms, including eleven bedrooms, *twenty-three* bathrooms, and five kitchens. The dining room floor is made of glass so that guests can view the indoor swimming pool beneath them.

‖‖

EACH STATE HAS ITS CHERISHED LANDMARKS, AND CAL-

ifornia is no exception. Here, however, what's cherished isn't something along the lines of Monticello, it's the Los Baños del Mar swimming pool. In 1992, it looked like the thirties pool and bathhouse would be destroyed to make way for yet another parking lot. The Santa Barbara City Council got hopping, however, and designated the pool a city landmark.

WHERE THERE'S RIGGS, THERE'S FIRE. THE DIRECTOR OF

Lethal Weapon 3 needed some spectacular pyrotechnics for his movie. The federal government needed to unload an abandoned housing development in Lancaster. The two got together and it was a deal that could only be struck in Hollywood. For $25,000, Warner Brothers got to destroy the fifty-four half-built homes that were deserted when the developer's S & L was seized by the feds. Ironically, the raging fire you saw in the movie was not the actual demise of the housing development. Moviemakers used carefully controlled propane gas lines to create the flames. The houses were bulldozed after the filming.

THE IMAGE OF CALIFORNIA AS A LAID-BACK, ANYTHING-

goes state is far from the truth. California homeowners are *pretty touchy* about their neighborhoods and absolutely rabid about their vistas. In Huntington Beach, Emad Ali Hassan's home exceeded height limits and blocked neighbors' views of the ocean. Hassan was ordered by the City Council to tear off the third story of his house. He is appealing the decision.

IT STARTED WITH A FEW CRACKS IN THE WALLS OF THE

Filipowiczes' new San Juan Capistrano home. Two months later, on a quiet Monday, a one-hundred-yard fissure in the hillside buckled the Filipowiczes' $300,000 custom-built home. As the gash widened, threatening to collapse the house, the Filipowiczes and their neighbor were forced to evacuate. The next day, the neighbors above the Filipowiczes watched as their patio broke apart and slid down the hill. Then their swimming pool broke away from its foundation, threatening four houses, including the Filipowiczes', which by this time was torn nearly in half. Three more families were evacuated. Authorities had no explanations.

GRAFFITI HAS LONG BEEN A PROBLEM IN LOS ANGELES.

The city spent more than $15 million in 1992 to clean up the messes left by graffiti artists desperate for attention. One of the sites targeted by the cleaning crews was most certainly the mayor's home. On a cinderblock wall next to Mayor Bradley's house, someone had used red spray paint to limn this message: "Don't Screw Us Tom."

FREEWAY LIVING

IN CALIFORNIA, YOU ARE WHAT YOU DRIVE. IN CASE you're thinking, well, I drive a Japanese import, that doesn't make me Japanese, I say, "Okay, I agree." (Smartass.) You should know, however, that in Mercedes/Rolls/Jaguar land, your sensible compact makes a statement, and that statement is, "I am predictable, stable, and boring. My life is going nowhere and the best I can hope for is behind me." A red Mercedes convertible, on the other hand, says, "I am well off, frivolous, and have a date every New Year's Eve." Which image would you rather project?

Now that you want to trade in your old car, let me give you a piece of advice: the best way to judge its statement value is to run it by the valet at the Regent Beverly Wilshire. I tried to park my brand-new Japanese import there once (I was meeting my agent for water). The valet just looked at me and said, "What?"

I knew then I could never turn my keys over to this man. Besides, I was embarrassed by my keyring—a secondhand shoe leather job with a cattle brand motif that I picked up at a crafts festival in my grandmother's church basement. Finally I found a parking lot in Glendale that would accept my car, then I hitchhiked back to Beverly Hills.

I'm not rich by any means, but I was determined to win over the valet at the Regent Beverly Wilshire. His approval became my raison d'être. I decided to check out the Mercedes dealership, hoping somehow that they would give me a great deal because I was such a nice person.

A man in a designer suit with discreet touches of gray in his tastefully styled hair asked if he might help me. Immediately, I was struck by the difference between this man and Coy Culpepper, the used-car salesman back home. In 1974, Coy, while wearing a lime-green leisure suit, sold both a Mercury Monarch AND a used Camaro in one day. He has worn that suit, and the white vinyl shoes, every day since.

The Mercedes salesman, who told me his name was Eaton, led me into the marble-floored showroom with its big potted palms. (I don't know why Californians equate palm trees with elegance. To me they look like giant pinecones with bad hair.) I was drawn immediately to the red convertible with black leather upholstery. The car was whispering, "No more sitting at home watching the ball drop at Times Square. You will have a date this New Year's Eve."

I mustered my courage and swallowed my pride. Exhausted by the effort, I squeaked, "How much does that model cost?" Eaton's shoulders sagged. He knew the old adage as well as I did: "If you have to ask . . ."

"This model," he sniffed, "costs $115,878.87."

I did some quick computations. If I were to get three extra jobs, sell my Dave Clark Five memorabilia collection, and never eat lunch again as long as I live, it would take me twenty-two years and eight months to pay this baby off.

"Thank you," I muttered and walked away, unable to bear Eaton's disappointment.

On the way home, as I squeezed my Japanese import between a Mercedes and a Rolls on the freeway, I found myself wondering if maybe, just maybe, Coy Culpepper might be free New Year's Eve.

IN CALIFORNIA, TRAFFIC VIOLATORS CAN REDUCE THEIR

penalties if they attend an eight-hour traffic school. L.A. has also reduced the boredom. DMV-approved classes are held by comics at the Improv, at a chocolate shop where speeders munch truffles while they learn the law, and over potluck dinners. One group of violators was given free lottery tickets.

ACCORDING TO THE CITY OF LOS ANGELES'S "TAXICAB

Drivers' Appearance Standards," trousers "shall be neither shorts nor cut-offs nor bib overalls nor leisure suits nor exercise (sweat) suits." The code also states unequivocally that "The body shall be without objectionable odors" and "Only women may wear skirts."

DURING THE SUMMER OF 1987, THERE WERE MORE THAN

twenty traffic-related shootings, including four fatalities, on L.A. freeways. One firm began offering car signs saying, PLEASE DON'T SHOOT.

FROM AN L.A. *TIMES* SURVEY OF SOUTHERN CALIFOR-

nians:

- Percentage who believe cars have ruined L.A.: 40%
- Percentage who have made an indecent gesture while driving: 40%
- Percentage involved in a traffic accident in the last year: 13%
- Percentage who believe it was the other guy's fault: 65%

A CALIFORNIA TERM WILL BE ADDED TO THE NEXT EDI-

tion of the *Oxford English Dictionary*. "SigAlert" refers to traffic jams with projected waits of thirty minutes or more. The term comes from Loyd C. Sigmon, a general manager of KMPC radio, who developed the radio warning service in the late fifties.

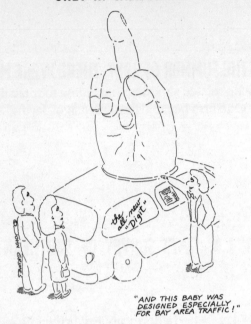

"AND THIS BABY WAS
DESIGNED ESPECIALLY
FOR BAY AREA TRAFFIC!"

ONE SUCH SIGALERT OCCURRED WHEN AUSTRALIAN AC-

tor Yahoo Serious chose rush hour to shoot a scene at the Citadel outlet mall next to the Santa Ana Freeway. Drivers stopped to gawk and before you could say "SigAlert," sixty thousand cars backed up fifteen miles, forcing motorists to wait for hours before they could begin moving again.

COMMUTING TIME IS SUCH A DRAG ON L.A. WORKERS'

energy that they are turning in earlier. Recognizing that a decline in ratings reflected a change in Southern California lifestyles, Channel 4 News moved its broadcast from 11:00 P.M. to 10:00 P.M. Freeway billboards read: NEWS CENTER 4 WILL NO LONGER AIR AT ELEVEN. DETAILS AT TEN.

ANOTHER *LOS ANGELES TIMES* POLL:

- Percentage of Southern Californians whose round-trip commute took one to two hours: 14%
- Percentage of Southern Californians whose round-trip commute took more than two hours: 5%
- Percentage who didn't know how long their commute took: 2%

CALIFORNIA LEGISLATORS PASSED A VERY UNPOPULAR

law among motorcycle enthusiasts that required them to wear helmets. A Santee woman dressed as a clown tried to explain that a helmet wouldn't fit over her fright wig; she was ticketed anyway. Another rider tried to get away with wearing a Tupperware bowl as protective gear.

PUH-LEASE. VON'S SUPERMARKET IN LA JOLLA OFFERS
valet parking for its customers.

AND DON'T CALL THEM METER MAIDS. OBJECTIVES OF
the California Association of Parking Controllers: "Primary objectives are to: unite parking controllers and obtain better benefits; educate the public about the duties of parking controllers while promoting and improving the public image of controllers. [The Association] Works for the passage of legislation requiring a 6–12 month jail sentence for persons convicted of assaulting a parking controller."

A GROUP OF THIRTEEN ELDERLY TOURISTS WHO HAD
just visited Disneyland were abandoned by their charter bus driver at a Bob's Big Boy in Santa Fe Springs. According to the police, witnesses said the driver "appeared to be under the influence of alcohol or narcotics or both." Santa Fe Springs donated the use of one of its vans to return the stranded tourists to their homes.

ON APRIL 3, 1990, ROBERT ALTON HARRIS WAS SCHED-

uled to be the first person executed in California in twenty-three years. Officials expected a huge turnout—of supporters and protestors—and changed the traditional 10:00 A.M. execution time to 3:00 A.M. to avoid traffic problems. The "traditional" time had been set in 1893, long before cars became a problem.

REAL MEN DON'T WEAR BIBS? THE 1992 GREATER LOS

Angeles Car Show featured a bunch of gadgets for those who live in their cars. One item was the D'Bab (Designed By A Blonde) Co.'s Auto Bib. It's a vinyl apron that protects the driver's chest and lap while he eats in the car. According to the designer, people like the apron after they put aside their egos and refuse to equate bibs with babies.

BUMPER STICKERS:

"I Stop for Men and Other Helpless Animals"
"Welcome to California. Now Go Home!"
"Fur: The Ultimate Sadist Symbol"
Spotted on a Cadillac: "We Are Refusing to Participate in the Recession"

"Real Men Eat Their Road Kill"
"I Love Animals: They're Delicious"
"I Brake for Auditions"
"I have PMS . . . and a handgun"

FORMER ACTRESS ELISABETH BROOKS AND PARTNER

Ernie Lipman run a chauffeur service for children of celebrities. A members-only service, Shlep-a-Ride has a fleet of thir-
teen cars and has toted the progeny of Beau Bridges and
Joanna Kerns.

FREEWAY BILLBOARDS:

THE 405 SHOULD BE THIS SMOOTH (whiskey ad)
MONEY IN THE BANK. IT'S LIKE THERAPY, ONLY CHEAPER. (bank ad)

SOUTHERN CALIFORNIA ROCK CLIMBERS HAVE CLAIMED

the freeway as their own: seventy-five rock-climbing walls have
been built on underpasses and bridges, and Caltrans (California Dept. of Transportation) is determined to dismantle each

and every one of them. One rock climber is not complaining; he hates artificial walls because, he explains, rocks are the "past thoughts of the gods solidified."

ACCORDING TO THE CALIFORNIA HIGHWAY PATROL,

"driving on an uncongested freeway requires at best only 5% of your attention." (Which goes a long way to explain why there are no uncongested freeways in California.)

AN ORANGE COUNTY LAWYER, MIFFED BECAUSE HE

had received three speeding tickets at the same spot, filed a lawsuit for $60 million under the RICO (Racketeer Influenced and Corrupt Organizations Act) statute. Ernest J. Franceschi, Jr. said Huntington Beach, by operating a speed trap on the

Pacific Coast Highway, extorted money from motorists. A U.S. district judge gave Franceschi the okay to proceed with his suit.

IN 1987, MICHAEL JOSEPH POMMERENING OF EUREKA

was ticketed for driving without a license and for letting his dog ride in the back of his pickup truck. Pommerening subsequently missed nine court appearances, which didn't set well with Judge Alan S. Rosenfield. P.O.'d, Rosenfield raised Pommerening's bail to the maximum: $99,999. His bail had originally been set at $198. The problem was bringing Pommerening in. Although he had been stopped four more times in Humboldt County for speeding and driving without insurance, the cops kept letting him go.

FROM A BERKELEY NEWSPAPER: PENIS ENVY AND LIGHT

RAILS TO BE EXPLORED. "The psychological underpinnings of developing rail transit will be the focus of a talk today on the UC Berkeley campus by transportation experts."

||||||||||||||||||||||||||||||||||||||||||||||||||||||||||||||||

BART MATTHEW LARSON, SEVENTEEN, WAS TICKETED

for driving 75 mph in a 55-mph zone. Larson elected to attend traffic school rather than pay the fine and returned to court with his certificate of completion. The traffic hearing officer said Larson was a day late and fined him $166.50. Larson didn't think that was fair, so he wrote a letter protesting the fine. Amazingly, without further impetus from Larson, the handwritten letter made its way through the judicial system all the way to the 4th District Court of Appeals—one step below the State Supreme Court. A three-judge panel reversed the hearing officer's decision and ordered that he dismiss the traffic ticket. The high court said a reprimand should have been enough punishment for Larson.

||||||||||||||||||||||||||||||||||||||||||||||||||||||||||||||||

A STRAY DOG WANDERED ONTO THE HARBOR FREEWAY

during rush hour traffic. Cars began backing up as the frantic puppy tried to find a way out. No problem, the California Highway Patrol stepped in and took control. As motorists watched in disbelief, the CHP officer ran over the dog.

||||||||||||||||||||||||||||||||||||||||||||||||||||||||||

ACCORDING TO A STUDY BY THE ROAD INFORMATION

program, California drivers waste 1.19 billion hours per year sitting in traffic. That breaks down to about 3½ days a year per person.

||||||||||||||||||||||||||||||||||||||||||||||||||||||||||

QUOTE FROM THE CALIFORNIA DMV ENVIRONMENTAL

(most states call them Vanity) License Plate booklet: "KEEP IT CLEAN" "Each request for Enviromental [sic] License Plates is . . . screened to prevent the issuance of a configuration that may be considered offensive or misleading. This difficult screening process entails the use of foreign language dictionaries, the Dictionary of American Slang . . . and the good judgment of the unit personnel making the decision whether or not to issue the requested configuration. The difficulty involved in making this decision is analogous to the U.S. Supreme Court's recurring attempts to determine standards of taste and decency upon which to base a definition of pornography."

||||||||||||||||||||||||||||||||||||||||||||||||||||||||||

THE CALIFORNIA DMV REQUIRES THAT MOTORIZED

wheelchair drivers must have drivers' licenses. In order to be licensed, applicants must pass a two-hour test. Disabled-rights activists questioned the wisdom of driving tests, asking, "What are they going to do if a person doesn't pass . . . impound his chair?"

WHEN THE GOLDEN GATE BRIDGE RAISED ITS RATES

from $2 to $3, Susan Deluxe of Marin County composed and recorded "I Got Ripped Off on My Way to San Francisco," performed to the tune of "I Left My Heart," etc. Deluxe makes sure the tape is blasting when she deposits her toll at the booth each morning.

ACCORDING TO THE *SAN FRANCISCO CHRONICLE*, ONE IN

five Bay Area residents feel traffic affects them more than any other issue, including drugs, crimes, and housing. (Three percent of those surveyed felt they had no problems.)

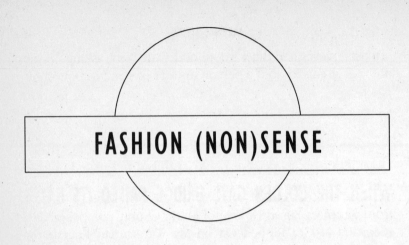

FASHION (NON)SENSE

WHEN APPLIED TO CALIFORNIANS, THE TERM "FASHION sense" is an oxymoron. One gander at the Academy Awards and you have to agree with me. Kim Basinger, soon to be installed in the Worst Dressed Hall of Fame, seems fond of gowns inspired by the Chicken-of-the-Sea mermaid. There are two categories of clothes on Oscar night: ugly and uglier. The truth is, if Earl Blackwell didn't exist, California would have to invent him.

Okay, that's Hollywood, you say, the same people who gave us Pia Zadora. Obviously, those folks have no sense, fashion or otherwise. What about the rest of the state?

The best explanation I can come up with for fashion outside of Hollywood is that Californians got tired of using their skin to support their internal organs, so they invented Spandex. Either that, or the Perfect Bodies wanted the rest of us to look like idiots when we followed suit.

To me, wearing bicycle shorts is a lot like wearing an inflated blood pressure cuff. Obviously, the two-hundred-and-fifty-pound woman I saw yesterday at the supermarket (Piggly Wiggly—isn't that appropriate?) disagreed with me. Those Spandex shorts bulged in so many places, it looked like she'd swallowed a set of radials.

Therein lies the problem. California starts a fashion trend and five to ten years later it makes its way across the country. The thing is, women in Pocatello, Idaho, probably should think twice before embracing a California fashion trend. I'm not saying women in Pocatello are not as attractive as California women, I'm just saying that imprudent use of California fashions can be hazardous.

There was one terrifying incident in which a woman in Winnemucca, Nevada, bought one of those little black Spandex numbers; you know, the dress with the hemline that hits just below your navel. She managed to squeeze into the thing, but it fit so tightly it cut off her circulation. The only way the Rescue Squad could pry her out of the dress was with the Jaws of Life.

This woman was not equipped to deal with California fashion. She expected to be able to wear the dress *and* maintain bodily functions. Women in California are more disciplined. They are able to go without food, oxygen, and rest stops for extended periods. Motion is optional. Before parties many women prefer to be placed in a strategic location, say in front of a mirror, where they will stand motionless and breathless until the last guest leaves. Sometimes CPR is involved.

A fashion trend now emerging in California has me a little

DOCTOR, BY DAY I'M A
FRUSTRATED NOB HILL MATRON,
BY NIGHT AN UNTAMED ANIMAL
PROWLING THE CLUBS IN
LIME-GREEN SPANDEX.
WHAT'S WRONG WITH ME?

FIRST THINGS
FIRST, ETHEL.
ARE YOU LICENSED
TO WEAR SPANDEX?

worried. Designers have transformed the little black Spandex dress. It still barely covers your navel, but it now resembles mummy wrap. If one of those babies were to spontaneously unwind, the recoil would hurl the wearer into hyperspace. The losses would be devastating. Unless, that is, we can convince Pia to try one on for size.

OWNERS OF VERTIGO, ONE OF L.A.'S TRENDY (IS THERE

another adjective for L.A.?) night spots, wanted to project an air of exclusivity, so customers were forced to wait in line à la Studio 54 until they were judged sartorially fit. Things got dicey when investigators from the Alcohol Beverage Control Department tried to enter the club to follow up on claims of clothes discrimination. The gatekeepers denied them admission because the investigators lacked "fashion sense." The Department sued. During the course of the trial, a former model and fashion consultant was a key witness for the defense. She declared that fashion is "fluid." She went on to say, "By the time you could publish a textbook on what is fashionable, the information would be outdated." To illustrate that fact, defense attorneys presented an article about the return to seventies disco styles.

IT HAS BEEN RUMORED, BUT NOT MEDICALLY PROVEN,

that when you move to L.A. your IQ drops ten points. To combat mental deficiencies, clubgoers have started drinking "smart drinks." Made from amino acids and oxygen, the drink comes in packet form, which can be mixed with fruit juice or mineral water and is supposed to improve brain functions. Like, sure.

IS NOTHING SACRED? THE JEWISH SHOP IN BEVERLY HILLS

sells hand-painted yarmulkes bearing the likenesses of Teenage Mutant Ninja Turtles, Sesame Street characters, and, yes, Bart Simpson.

IN L.A., WHERE THE COLOR OF ONE'S EYES IS OFTEN HID-

den behind shades, it seems only natural (to Californians) that the Los Angeles Craft and Folk Art Museum features a collection of glasses—sun and eye—dating from 1940.

EVEN STRANGER IS THE LOS ANGELES COUNTY MUSEUM

of Art's 1992 exhibit of shoes designed by Salvatore Ferragamo.

A T-SHIRT DESIGNER IN HOLLYWOOD, STANLEY DESANTIS,

during the economic downslide of 1992, brought out a line of "Recession Wear—Clothes for the Downwardly Mobile." His slogan: "How to Lose Your Shirt and Still Be Fashionable."

WRETCHED EXCESS: RONI ZEE'S CLOTHING STORE, AT THE

Crocker Galleria in San Francisco, offers a $5,000 men's tie. The tie is made from navy silk and studded with gold and diamonds.

FROM AN ADVERTISEMENT:

"Q: Is it proper to wear Lee sweats to your wedding?"
"A: Yes, but only if you live in California."

LET THEM WEAR NIKES. IN OCTOBER 1991, THE FOOT

Locker athletic footware store gave away over one thousand pairs of Nikes and Reeboks to L.A.'s homeless. Most of the recipients were grateful for the donation; others tried to sell the shoes as soon as they walked out the mission doors.

IF YOU WERE WONDERING ... BULLOCK'S WILSHIRE HAS

been designated by historians as the first suburban department store. The company's foresighted founders built the store in a bean field in 1929.

WHAT'S IN AND WHAT'S NOT CHANGES BY THE MINUTE

in L.A. At one time, the hot spot was Club-Sin-A-Matic, popular with the leather and tattoo crowd. Special events drew the crowds. At one, a drag queen applied pancake syrup and whipped cream to a man's feet, then licked it off.

THE FASHION OF CHOICE IN L.A. (FOR A TIME) WAS BASIC

black and a string of pearls . . . for men. Often worn with combat boots, the lustrous white looked lovely against black T-shirts.

PALM SPRINGS MAYOR SONNY BONO, APPALLED BY THE

skimpy swimsuits worn by the spring break college crowd, pushed through a law which read: "No person shall appear, bathe, sunbathe, dress or undress, or ride in or on any vehicle . . . in such a manner that the genitals, pubic hair, buttocks, anus, anal regions, natal cleft . . . or any portion of the breast at or below the upper edge of the areola thereof of any female person, is exposed to public view." Sonny says the law was passed to get rid of thong bathing suits. Dare we ask, could this law be designed to get rid of Cher as well?

If we are going to have judges at fashion shows, let's put some teeth into the law.

EARL BLACKWELL'S "TEN WORST-DRESSED" LISTS ARE

a Hollywood staple. Mr. Blackwell is not amused, however, when the shoe, shall we say, is on the other foot. After Johnny Carson mentioned in his monologue that Blackwell had put Mother Teresa on his worst-dressed list, Mr. Blackwell initiated an $11 million defamation of character lawsuit. A judge dismissed the case, saying Johnny's joke was harmless.

WHAT IS THIS THING WITH FEET? AT THE BISTRO GARDEN

in L.A., Claudio Merazzi's shoes were not worn by models but were carried through the invitation-only audience on silver trays. The centerpiece at each table was a Merazzi slipper resting on a blue velvet pillow.

THE DRESS CODE FOR WOMEN EMPLOYEES OF THE NEW-

hall Branch of the Bank of America states that "undergarments: bra, slip, panties, and nylons are a must at all times." Who, may we ask, is checking for compliance?

FROM A FLYER: "HAVE YOU SEEN THIS SOCK? LAST SEEN

in laundromat on 4th and Redondo. Was favorite pair—black, cotton blend—elastic bands—size 9–11. If found, PLEASE RETURN!"

PUH-LEASE. THE CALIFORNIA LEGISLATURE HAS DESIG-

nated Speedo swimwear as "the official swimwear of the Los Angeles County lifeguards."

IN ANOTHER, ALBEIT POLITICALLY INCORRECT, ACT OF

charity, Bizakis Fur of Orange County donated thirty fur coats
to homeless women, never stopping to think, we're sure, that
the money those coats cost could have bought the women a
home.

THE EIGHTIES ARE DEAD, PACK UP YOUR CHIC AND GO

home. According to the *Los Angeles Times* society editor, the
nineties Hollywood parties are "reality-in-your-face benefits
drawing socially conscious guests who are careful not to wear
furs or arrive in limos. The point here is not just to hear about
people suffering but to represent it."

JAMIE REIDY OF LOS ANGELES HAS COME UP WITH THE

ultimate status symbol: a twelve-inch, gold-plated grocery cart.
Selling price: $1,000. Reidy calls his carts Dream Keepers and
has sold over 15,000 of them.

CARTIER'S SIGNATURE CIGARETTE MADE ITS AMERICAN

debut on Rodeo Drive. The store even offered by-the-carton home delivery service for major credit card holders. In 1989, the upscale smokes sold for $3 a pack—nearly two times the going rate for regular ones. When he heard about the debut, the head of an antismoking lobby asked, "What are Cartier smokers going to get—cancer at twice the price?"

AND MORE WRETCHED EXCESS: THEODORE'S ON RODEO

Drive kept a one-piece, multicolored, sequined bodysuit on display at the store's entrance. Price: $6,000.00. Ridiculously overpriced, you say? Not for the women who shop at Theodore's. The store's ad slogan sums up its clientele: "I always get what I want."

TO SHOW HIS CONCERN FOR CHEETAHS AND OTHER EN-

dangered animals, Kenton Faust of Irvine shaved the hair around his temples and painted cheetah spots on them. For six months, Faust's employer, PacTel, put up with the spots but finally laid down the law. Faust covered the spots with white shoe polish but is on the lookout for a lawyer. He doesn't think the cheetah look is in violation of PacTel's dress code, which simply states that employees must be "neatly groomed."

|||||||||||||||||||||||||||||||||||||||||||||||||||||||||||||

SO YOU THOUGHT THOSE DISNEY PEOPLE ARE A BUNCH

of creative free spirits? Not so. The company dress code not only discourages "clinging fabrics," but also forbids sideburns below the earlobes, heavy perfume, earrings larger than a penny, facial hair, dark red nail polish, and Earth Shoes.

|||||||||||||||||||||||||||||||||||||||||||||||||||||||||||||

JOSE EBER (PRONOUNCED JOE-ZAY—HE'S FRENCH), HAIR-

dresser to the stars, gets $200 a whack at his Rodeo Drive salon. Eber's regulars include Liz Taylor, Cher, George Hamilton (would someone please tell me what this man does for a living?), and Tom Selleck. Jose is so popular he will not accept new clients. Why would anyone pay $200 for a trim? According to Pia Zadora (definitely my choice for the last word in fashion), "Jose doesn't just *cut* the hair; he *sculpts* it."

|||||||||||||||||||||||||||||||||||||||||||||||||||||||||||||

FIRST, THERE WAS MADONNA RUNNING AROUND IN HER

skivvies. Now, at this moment, and subject to change in the next, men in California are showing us their underwear. Some men, however, balk at the form-fitting stretchies, and according to L.A. designer Drew Bernstein, "A lot of people say [the stretch knits] are too much like leotards and it's a ballerina look. But I don't see it that way at all. I see it as a Robin Hood style." Perhaps men would feel more comfortable in the tell-alls if designers would include a pair of rolled-up socks with each purchase?

WHERE ELSE WOULD ANYONE GIVE SERIOUS THOUGHT

(or column inches) to Michael Jackson's video attire? After Jackson's "Remember the Time" video debuted on MTV, a California fashion critic described Michael's costumes as "antique Egyptian with street-edge funk" and actually wondered if teens would adopt the look. Forgive me, but I have a hard time imagining a fourteen-year-old hormone-ravaged boy wearing "what appears to be a skirt, thigh boots, and a bra that looks like a metallic harness."

CHERYL SHUMAN IS OPTICIAN TO THE STARS. NOW THAT

smart is "in," Hollywood stars are clamoring for glasses. Even those, like Paula Abdul, who have perfect eyesight. Shuman has also done the eyeglasses for movies, including *Pretty Woman, Thelma and Louise,* and *Terminator II.* (Funny, I don't remember Arnold wearing glasses.) The optician has become so indispensable that actor Robert Downey, Jr. demanded that she stay on the set to fit his glasses for *Soapdish.* For this, Shuman got $20,000 for ten days' work.

CALIFORNIA CUISINE:

101 USES FOR A DEAD SQUID

FOR MY LAST BIRTHDAY, A MISGUIDED FRIEND GAVE ME
a California cookbook. Since I no longer live in California, she thought I must miss the food. I don't. I miss California cuisine about as much as I miss my third-grade teacher—the one who plucked her chin hairs at her desk. Nevertheless, I gushed and said I would have the gift-giver over *soon* for an authentic California meal. "Okay," she said. "How about Tuesday?"

Well, I thought, I'll make the best of a bad situation. Pick something simple, light, and tasty with ingredients readily available at my local grocer's. I glanced through the book, confidently at first, then with increasing dismay. Obviously my friend had not read it, or she had forgotten that we live in a small southern town where the grocery's gourmet section consists of fruit roll-ups and pitted prunes.

Chapter One was entitled "All About Squid." I skipped that one. Chapter Two: "Pizza." All right, pizza, this is good. The introduction said, "In order to make this pizza, you must have baking tiles made from Tuscan clay which have been fired at 1200° for exactly seven minutes." Okay, next chapter.

Once I passed pizza, I found myself in delicacy world. The menus sounded like they were concocted by an eight-year-old boy who slept with worms: avocado ice cream, tofu burritos, green-lipped mussel soup. Here we have crawfish, we have bottom suckers, and we have shad. We do not have green-lipped mussels, we do not have mussels of any ilk, and if we did you would not see a single one of us drawing close enough to determine its lip color.

"Bubba, you got you a good one there. You gotta throw it back. Blue lips. Tough break, buddy."

I persevered and settled on a menu. Now to assemble the ingredients. I called my grocer.

"Do you have any arugula?" I asked. Silence.

"Arugula, do you have any?" I repeated.

"Lady, are you choking? Or is this an obscene phone call?"

"No, no, arugula," I said, "it's a salad green. Oh, never mind. How about fennel?"

"Funnel? Yeah, we got funnels. Aisle seven, kitchenware."

I pressed on.

"Kiwi?"

"Aisle five, shoe polish."

"Pasta dyed with squid ink?"

Silence.

"Shitake mushrooms?"

"Gesundheit."

At this point, I gave up. Intuition told me that I was wasting my time and risking public ridicule.

"See that lady over there? She actually thinks sausage comes from ducks."

"No!"

"Really, it's true. The grocer told me."

My friend came for dinner. She found on her plate a dab of tuna salad, a dab of squished pinto beans, and a wedding cookie smeared with raspberry jam. I had curled the parsley garnish with my electric rollers to make it look exotic. My friend took one look at her plate and excused herself, saying she had to use the ladies' room. After several minutes passed and she hadn't returned, I started looking for her. Obviously, she had climbed out the bathroom window. I haven't seen her since.

L.A.'S MOST EXPENSIVE RESTAURANT IS GINZA SUCHI KO,

where the average tuna belly, sea eel, or sea urchin dinner runs $125 to $150 per person (without cocktails). You may find it hard to make a reservation, however—Ginza has an unlisted telephone number.

FOR $100, MILLIGAN'S IN LA JOLLA OFFERS A GOURMET

hot dog for two served with a bottle of Dom Perignon. As of 1991, the meal had been ordered seven times.

© RICHARD GUINDON, 1983

"It's a piece of pineapple, a slice of orange and some grapes. They do that in California where people still know how to take chances."

▌ Presentation is everything: One restaurant offers "salmon in soba noodles served lukewarm on glass bricks."

▌ Presentation is nothing: Rafael's Royal Thai restaurant offers grilled squid on a stick.

L.A.'S POSHEST RESTAURANTS (L'ERMITAGE, MAPLE

Drive, et al.) got together and created "Dial-A-Dinner." For an additional 20 percent charge, tuxedo-clad waiters will deliver menu items to your front door. (That is, if your front door is in Beverly Hills, Brentwood, or one of the other acceptable L.A. neighborhoods.)

THE ORIGINAL BEACHCOMBER RESTAURANT IN HOLLY-

wood served the likes of Gary Cooper, and in 1934 its bar-tender, Donn Beach, created the ubiquitous Mai Tai and Zombie cocktails.

THOSE "DING DONGS" ARE GONNA COST YOU. IN 1991,

in an effort to bring the state budget under control, the California legislature levied a "snack tax" on previously exempt junk food. There is some confusion, however, on the definition of a "snack." For example, the prepackaged miniature pecan pie you take home from the convenience store is a snack. But that slice of pecan pie slipped into a styrofoam container from the deli—that's nontaxable food.

TRENDY TULIPE RESTAURANT MIXES THE MEAT FROM A

pig's foot with snails, brains, and sweetbreads (aka pancreas), wraps the concoction in fat, and fries it. There are people in California who pay to eat this.

AH, AMBIENCE: EDDIE JACK'S IN SAN FRANCISCO IS DECO-
rated with papier-mâché beer cans and cigarette packs.

THERE IS NO REST FOR THE WEARY AND NO BREAK FOR
the consumer. Ad execs in California came up with a new way to invade consumers' homes: advertisements on eggshells. "You can't ignore it when you open the refrigerator," said Rafi Orel, president of Golden Eggs. "It's shouting at you, 'Here I am!' "

C. C. BROWN'S IN L.A. CLAIMS TO HAVE INVENTED THE
hot fudge sundae in 1906.

DURING THE DESERT STORM CRISIS, BARNEY STONE PUB
in San Diego offered "Nuclear Meltdown Specials," which included a patty melt or tuna melt topped with a mushroom cap.

COLIN COOPER OF SANTA BARBARA IS BETTING ON THE

future with his ostrich ranch. Since 1990, Cooper has been breeding and raising ostriches—not for their feathers, not for their eggs, not for their aesthetic value and kid appeal, but for meat. Hoping that California health consciousness holds out, Cooper predicts that his low-fat white-meat ostriches will be a hit among the tofu crowd.

CALIFORNIA IS THE WORLD'S LARGEST PRUNE PRO-

ducer, responsible for 70 percent of all prunes grown.

EVEN TRADER VIC'S JUMPED ON THE OCCULT BAND-

wagon in the seventies. For a time, the Beverly Hills restaurant stored its wine inside a pyramid, claiming that the structure's magic powers improved the quality of even the most unassuming wine.

CALIFORNIA, INCREASINGLY MUSHROOM CRAZY, PERHAPS

found its soul mate in *lactarius deliciosus*, a French mushroom that when cut bleeds orange. This delicacy is offered at La Toque in West Hollywood.

ACCORDING TO A *LOS ANGELES TIMES* REVIEW OF

Meshulam Riklis's (husband of Pia Zadora) new restaurant, "the french fries were downright paradigmatic."

IN 1990, THE USDA RULED THAT SEBASTOPOL-AREA

chickens raised and marketed by Bart and Pat Ehrman could no longer be labeled as "Rocky the Range Chicken" because the Department of Agriculture did not recognize the term "range." The Ehrmans allow their chickens to run free, feed them soy products, and do not use hormones on their fowl. Feeling that their $4-million-a-year business was threatened because of the ruling, Ms. Ehrman said, "We can't use the word organic, we can't use the word range, we can't say the birds are vegetarian fed. I guess we can still use the word chicken."

P.S. In a stunning reversal, USDA officials gave back to the Ehrmans the word "range." The decision meant that the Ehrmans were free to use their "Rocky the Range Chicken" logo: a chicken in a six-gallon hat clutching a gun.

IN ADDITION TO THE $5.2 MILLION SAMMY DAVIS, JR.

owed the IRS when he died in May 1990, he also owed Von's grocery $35,000 for groceries he had charged.

DURING THE 1990 PERRIER WATER CRISIS, WHEN IT WAS

discovered that the popular mineral water was contaminated with benzene, California's second-largest mineral water bottler was forced to add another shift at its plant to keep up with demand. Californians drink 40 percent of the bottled water sold in the United States.

ACCORDING TO THE *SAN FRANCISCO EXAMINER*, IN ONE

week at training camp the 49ers eat:

25 boxes of cereal
100 gallons of milk
150 loaves of bread
200 gallons of lemonade
200 pounds of seafood
500–1,000 pounds of potatoes
500 pounds of cooked pasta

500 pounds of beef
500 pounds of vegetables
600–700 pounds of poultry
800 pounds of fruit
90 dozen eggs

A NEW TASTE SENSATION AT ST. ESTEPHE IN MANHATTAN

Beach is chocolate chili ice cream. According to owner John Sedlar, when you take a bite, "First you taste sweet, then bitter and cold. A couple of seconds later—the hot surprise." But do you take a second bite?

NOT TO BE OUTDONE, BERKELEY'S 4TH STREET GRILL

serves up *mole* pound cake with chiles, roasted tomatoes, pumpkin seeds, and semisweet chocolate, covered with chocolate sauce.

AND WHILE WE'RE ON THE SUBJECT OF CHOCOLATE, CHEF

Pierre Herme at San Francisco's Meridien Hotel once offered an all-chocolate dinner that included:

a chocolate rum aperitif
chocolate scrambled eggs
chocolate tart
fried chocolate peaches
chocolate sherbert
chocolate cheese bananas
chocolate raspberry macaroons
Top this off with chocolate coffee and chocolate truffles. Perhaps the meal should be billed as the PMS Special.

JULIE'S RESTAURANT BRAGS THAT IT IS L.A.'S ONLY

restaurant–carwash.

ARSENIO HALL TRIED IT AND PRONOUNCED IT A TREND:

the Tequila Sucker with a Worm. For under $2.00 (1991 prices) you can have one of Larry Peterman's suckers. Made from alcohol-free ingredients that surround an authentic red worm commonly found floating at the bottom of tequila bottles, the sucker sounds disgusting. But if you must, Peterman, who also has banana and jalapeño suckers, has a toll-free number: 1-800-EAT-WORM.

THE HOSTESS FOR THANKSGIVING DINNER WAS ELVIRA,

Mistress of the Dark. In attendance were River Phoenix, Rue McClanahan, k.d. lang, and Patti Davis. The guest of honor was a turkey. Not to be eaten, mind you, but fêted. These animal lovers, in defiance of Pilgrim tradition, ate tofu pot pie.

ACCORDING TO A NATIONWIDE SURVEY CONDUCTED BY

Domino's Pizza, California is the least health-conscious state (meat is the most-requested topping), and Californians are the worst tippers.

IN ITS SIXTY-FOUR-YEAR HISTORY, THE ORIGINAL PANTRY

in downtown L.A. has been open twenty-four hours a day, 365 days a year, and has never missed serving a meal.

WHEN THE MARRIOTT CORPORATION TOOK OVER THE

concessions at Dodger Stadium, it replaced the traditional grilled hot dogs with steamed franks. Irate Dodger fans boycotted the stadium. One hot dog purist, and Kevin Costner fan, stated his terms, "If they grill them, we will come."

GARLIC RUSTLING HAS GOTTEN SO OUT OF HAND IN GIL-

roy, Garlic Capital of the World, that the sheriff's department has assigned a man full-time to patrol the fields. Rustlers caught with three or more grocery sacks full of garlic face grand theft felony charges. In 1990, more than two tons of garlic were stolen from Gilroy farms.

IN ORDER TO SATISFY WEIGHT-OBSESSIVE SOUTHERN

Californians, restaurants such as Le Petit Four and Marie Callender's have added Ultra Slim-Fast to their menus. Le Petit Four charges $3.00 each for the diet shake.

IN CALIFORNIA IT ISN'T ALWAYS WHAT YOU EAT BUT

what you do with the leftovers. In Ojai, city employees feed some fifteen pounds of scraps daily to the 2,500 worms kept in a box outside City Hall. The worms digest the garbage, turning it into a rich fertilizer. The planners hope the idea catches on and that "vermiculture" becomes a part of everyone's life. According to one proponent, a worm box could be used even in an efficiency apartment, perhaps doubling as a window seat.

SOUTHERN CALIFORNIA RESTAURANTS USING WOOD

fires to cook their barbecue could not meet air emission standards. Not that they didn't try. One restaurant owner spent $65,000 on equipment, but it couldn't handle the grease and smoke. While some officials argued that the fifty or fewer restaurants contributed little to L.A.'s smog, the South Coast Air Quality Management District continued to insist on compliance. Trying not to be the bad guys, the AQMD hired a consulting firm to come up with some answers to the pit barbecue problem. Cost of the consultant's study: $125,000.

THE LOS ANGELES COUNTY HISTORICAL LANDMARKS AND

Records Commission designated Bob's Big Boy Restaurant in Burbank an official "California Point of Historical Interest." According to Commission members, the forty-three-year-old restaurant is an example of "early coffee shop design," which originated in L.A. One patron suggested that any building in Los Angeles that lasted over forty years deserved to be made into a shrine.

THIS ADVICE TO CUSTOMERS FROM A SPAGO WAITER:

"You never want to piss off the person who is handling what you are putting in your mouth."

TUMMY TUCKS & HEAD SHRINKS:

HEALTH AND BEAUTY

||||||||||||||||||||||||||||||||||||||||||||||||||||||||||

I WAS A PERFECT TEN ONCE. OKAY, IT WAS AT BIRTH and I rated high on the Apgar scale. Since then the best I've been able to manage was a weak five. I've been too skinny, too fat, too short, too tall, too flat-chested, too busty, too hippy, and too hipless, according to the prevailing fashion. Have I ever considered plastic surgery? Never. I hate pain and I hate my bad luck. I wash my car, it rains. I get my boobs done, there's a Twiggy renaissance. Simple law of physics.

And then there's my friend Barbara, a key grip who lives in Malibu. Barbara has had two nose jobs (the second one refined her nostril flare); she has had her eyes done, her butt tucked, her boobs lifted. She has been liposuctioned, injected, and plumped. There isn't a verb in the plastic surgery lexicon that can't be applied to this woman.

Barbara has face-lifts like the rest of us have mammograms: the first one at thirty-five, then one every five years. I told her, if they keep pulling on her skin, her boobs will end up on her shoulders.

"Fine," she hissed, "then I won't have to wear shoulder pads."

I realized things had gotten completely out of hand when I caught Barb studying her face in the mirror. (Actually, Barbara is always studying her face in the mirror. This day she just looked more disgusted than usual.)

"Oh, I look awful," she said. "My philtral ridges are all wrong."

"Your what?"

"Philtral ridges," she said, and pointed to those two little vertical lines that run from your nose to your lips.

"They look okay to me," I said stupidly, expecting this pronouncement to satisfy her plastic surgery bloodlust.

"They're too long, my hairdresser told me the other day. He said he couldn't in good conscience let me go around with my philtral ridges out of kilter."

"Your hairdresser, the white guy with purple Rasta braids? Why, may I ask, was he staring at your philtral ridges?"

"That's just it, he wasn't staring. He said they jump out at you."

"Perhaps, then, you should take them for obedience training. Oh, come on, Barb, this is ridiculous. You look fine."

"Fine is not a compliment," she sniffed, "I'm calling Dr. Deep-Pockets. I heard he did Frank Gifford's face-lift. If he's good enough for Kathy Lee's man, he's good enough for me."

"Barbara, you're talking about a woman who married Frank Gifford and works with Regis Philbin. I wouldn't put a whole lot of faith in her judgment. Maybe you should give this a little more thought."

"I have given it thought, I've made up my mind. I'm going for the ridge lift." Barb paused and gave me a long searching look.

"Why don't you go with me," she said. "Maybe Dr. Deep-Pockets could do something about your jawline."

"My jawline, what's wrong with my jawline? I have a perfectly good jawline."

"It's blurring."

"Blurring, what do you mean blurring?"

"You know, dewlaps. Like your mother."

I looked in the mirror. My God, I thought, it's true.

Once my face had more angles than Linda Hamilton's; now there were these soft little rolling hills and dewlaps. Standing there looking into the mirror, I no longer saw myself, I saw instead MY MOTHER.

"Barb," I sighed, "do you think Dr. D. takes MasterCard?"

▌▌▌

IN 1988, THE MISS AMERICA PAGEANT PEOPLE HAD

a cow when they learned that Miss San Diego officials had named Dr. Stephen P. Grifka to serve as the San Diego pageant's "official plastic surgery consultant." According to Grifka's contract, he would inform contestants about plastic surgery options that could "enhance" their appearance. Grifka admitted, however, that there are limits to what he can do. "I can't change a couch into a chair. But I can certainly fluff up the pillows."

MISS WHITTIER 1988 WAS FIRED BECAUSE SHE ENTERED

a strip bikini pageant the night after she won her crown. Pageant officials felt that kind of exposure didn't help Whittier's image.

MOST OF US WHO HAVE THOUGHT TWICE ABOUT PLASTIC

surgery usually think breast enhancement, face-lifts, nose jobs. Not Susan Ruttan of "L.A. Law." Ms. Ruttan had her knees liposuctioned because they were "fat and round." Excuse me, but what shape are knees supposed to be?

THE L'ERMITAGE HOTEL IN BEVERLY HILLS HAS A SEPA-

rate wing for celebrities recovering from plastic surgery. It even offers a chauffeured limousine for rides to and from the hospital. The celebrities are whisked to their rooms via L'Ermitage's secret underground entrance. For around $400 a night, the hotel offers round-the-clock nurses, and soft food for those recovering from face-lifts.

|||||||||||||||||||||||||||||||||||||||||||||||||||||||||||||

ACCORDING TO "TV GUIDE," SINGER/ACTOR KENNY ROG-

ers admits that he has been liposuctioned three times—twice to reduce stomach fat, the last time to streamline his chin. Unfortunately for Rogers, after the chin job his beard started to grow behind his ears. How attractive.

|||||||||||||||||||||||||||||||||||||||||||||||||||||||||||||

ACCORDING TO COLUMNIST ROBERT A. JONES OF THE *LOS*

Angeles Times, a friend who was flying back to L.A. was seated next to a very attractive woman. They had a couple of drinks, a couple of laughs. He was feeling pretty good about the situation when the woman turned to him and asked for a favor. It seems she had just had her breasts augmented but was worried that her boyfriend would think they felt strange. Would he please feel them and tell her if they felt natural? He did, they did. They both were happy.

|||||||||||||||||||||||||||||||||||||||||||||||||||||||||||||

IT'S NOT UNUSUAL FOR UNHAPPY PATIENTS TO SUE DOC-

tors. But Jodie Bullock didn't stop there. When her breast enhancement was botched, she sued an L.A. TV station for running a favorable profile of the plastic surgeon she subsequently chose to do the surgery. The suit alleged that the surgeon in question was under investigation for drug and alcohol abuse and that the satisfied client shown in the profile was not a patient but the surgeon's girlfriend.

||||||||||||||||||||||||||||||||||||||||||||||||||||||

THY NAME IS VANITY. WOMEN WHO WERE NOT EN-

dowed with full lips like Michelle Pfeiffer or Kim Basinger flocked to plastic surgeons to have their lips "plumped" with collagen. Injectable collagen was developed by Collagen Corporation in Palo Alto. Over 760,000 people worldwide have used the shots to fill out lips, smooth out wrinkles, and eliminate scars. A full 18 percent (136,800 patients) of Collagen Corporation's business comes from Southern California. One Beverly Hills dermatologist says he alone has injected more than thirty thousand patients.

||||||||||||||||||||||||||||||||||||||||||||||||||||||

ONE BEVERLY HILLS PLASTIC SURGEON ESTIMATES THAT

65 percent of his clients are men. Most popular procedures: pectoral implants, calf implants, and yes, face-lifts.

||||||||||||||||||||||||||||||||||||||||||||||||||||||

THE LOS ANGELES GROUP FOR PSYCHOTHERAPY PRO-

vides one-stop shopping. They advertise services for "pre & post operative trauma counseling" for cosmetic surgery candidates. So you *can* get your head shrunk for your tummy tuck at one convenient location.

||||||||||||||||||||||||||||||||||||||||||||||||||||||

BEDFORD DRIVE IN BEVERLY HILLS IS KNOWN AS "COUCH

Canyon." About two hundred therapists have offices there.

||||||||||||||||||||||||||||||||||||||||||||||||||||||

DR. RICHARD ROSENTHAL, A THERAPIST WHO HAS OFFICES

in Beverly Hills and West L.A., turned his interest in Fyodor Dostoyevsky's compulsive gambling into a lucrative practice. Rosenthal treats people who share Dostoyevsky's compulsion. One patient would bet on anything, including which raindrop ran down the windowpane faster.

||||||||||||||||||||||||||||||||||||||||||||||||||||||

THE HERMOSA BEACH YELLOW PAGES HAS A LISTING FOR

ANXIETY.

||||||||||||||||||||||||||||||||||||||||||||||||||||||

WHEN SAN JOSE ASSEMBLYMAN JOHN VASCONCELLOS

suffered a heart attack, he decided to try a New Age treatment. In a letter to his constituents, Vasconcellos asked them to imagine they were traveling through his cholesterol-clogged arteries, sweeping away the health-threatening deposits.

||||||||||||||||||||||||||||||||||||||||||||||||||||||

TWO OFFICERS INVOLVED IN THE BEATING OF RODNEY

King filed worker's compensation claims citing "acute stress and anxiety."

||||||||||||||||||||||||||||||||||||||||||||||||||||||

IN SAN ANSELMO, ADVOCATES FOR THE ELDERLY SUB-

mitted a proposal to the Marin County Board of Supervisors to get approval to build a research center on aging. When the board members saw that the center would do research on "rats, mice, slugs, and worms," they were troubled. Before they would approve the plans, board members ordered a $6,000 study done to determine the effects animal research would have on the community's self-esteem.

||||||||||||||||||||||||||||||||||||||||||||||||||||

TWO THOUSAND STUDENTS FROM THE SANTA MONICA-

Malibu school district gathered in 1989 at the Santa Monica
Civic Auditorium for the fortieth annual "Stairway of the Stars"
musical performance. Shortly after the program began, the
female sopranos—sixteen of them—fainted. Within minutes,
247 of the performers—male and female—fell ill, complaining
of headaches, dizziness, and nausea. Nineteen students were
taken to emergency rooms. Following an investigation in which
environmental toxins were ruled out, a group of UCLA psychiatrists determined that the illnesses were caused by mass
hysteria. This affliction, one of the psychiatrists explained, dates
back to the Middle Ages, "when there were outbreaks of un-
usual behaviors in isolated groups, like in nunneries. There
was a cat-mewing incident—the nuns mewed like cats."

||||||||||||||||||||||||||||||||||||||||||||||||||||

AFTER TWENTY-TWO YEARS WITH THE LOS ANGELES CITY

Fire Department, Captain Michael J. Kaemmerer decided to
become Captain Michele. The department stood behind Kaemmerer's decision. Sensitivity sessions conducted by the department psychiatrist helped Kaemmerer's fellow firefighters
adjust to the change. Kaemmerer is now one of the highest-
ranking women in the department.

||||||||||||||||||||||||||||||||||||||||||||||||||||||||

A THIRTY-SEVEN-YEAR-OLD MENTAL HEALTH PROFES-

sional was feeling a little down in the dumps when she saw a TV ad for free counseling. She called the toll-free number and was told to come to a hospital in Long Beach. When the woman arrived and it was determined that her insurance would foot the bill, she was forcibly moved and committed to a psychiatric ward. Her lawyers managed to have her released after one night. Later she received a bill from the hospital for $1,700.

||||||||||||||||||||||||||||||||||||||||||||||||||||||||

HEADLINE IN THE *HERMOSA BEACH DAILY BREEZE*: MILI-

TARY MEN LEAVE SPERM BEHIND BEFORE DEPARTING.

||||||||||||||||||||||||||||||||||||||||||||||||||||||||

FROM THE CLASSIFIEDS:

| "NON-SURGICAL FACE LIFT $10. Discover the Fountain of Youth. Complete line of the best skin care products including the favorite of film stars & models, *glacial marine mud*."

| "Toucher La Forme. The incomparable French technique of total relaxation. . . . Stunning young Gymnast. Unique —Exclusive."

||||||||||||||||||||||||||||||||||||||||||||||||

ACCORDING TO CBS NEWS, A RECENT STUDY FOUND THAT

eight out of ten girls under the age of ten in San Francisco had been on a diet.

||||||||||||||||||||||||||||||||||||||||||||||||

FROM A HERMOSA BEACH YELLOW PAGES AD: "PERMA-

nent make-up made legal. Torrance City Council voted to allow 'Hairline' to practice permanent make-up, a procedure to permanently darken eyebrows, underline eyes, and outline lips." Next to the ad is a photograph of the store owner *and her attorney*.

||||||||||||||||||||||||||||||||||||||||||||||||

TRACY WIERMAN OF REDDING WAS A DISCIPLINED RUN-

ner, but when she exercised she started having violent reactions: her eyes swelled shut, she sneezed repeatedly, her airways constricted, she vomited. After a series of tests, Tracy's allergist concluded that she was allergic to aerobic activity. In order to preserve her health, Tracy gave up running and took up skydiving instead.

||||||||||||||||||||||||||||||||||||||||||||||||||||||

AN OAKLAND WOMAN'S AGED CAT SUDDENLY BECAME

aggressive and insecure, so she took it to the Campanile Veterinary Clinic for acupuncture treatments. There it was determined that the cat's *chi* had been blocked. Acupuncture unstuck it, and according to the owner the cat is once again "relaxed."

||||||||||||||||||||||||||||||||||||||||||||||||||||||

GONE ARE THE TWO-MARTINI LUNCHES. GONE ARE THE

sprout and mineral water lunches. Heck, lunch is gone altogether. Busy executives in San Francisco do deals while jogging along the Embarcadero, over a massage, or during a game of squash. According to one executive, "You can gain a lot by having someone on court sucking wind."

||||||||||||||||||||||||||||||||||||||||||||||||||||||

FIVE WORKERS AT THE MERRITT PERALTA MEDICAL CEN-

ter in Oakland suddenly began losing their hair. Four of those hit by the strange malady were women who developed bald spots on their scalps. The male worker's hair got so thin he shaved it and started wearing a hat. Authorities were at a loss to explain the source of the affliction. Could it, we wonder, have anything to do with cat mewing?

||||||||||||||||||||||||||||||||||||||||||||||||||||||||||

FEAR OF PREMATURE WRINKLES HAS MADE TANS PASSÉ

in Hollywood. One screenwriter's date was so afraid of burning rays that she wore a beekeeper's hat and veil to the beach.

||||||||||||||||||||||||||||||||||||||||||||||||||||||||||

CALIFORNIA HAS A LONG HISTORY OF WAY-OUT REME-

dies. Gaylord Wilshire of the Boulevard fame developed a magnetic collar which, he claimed, would return gray hair to its natural color. This leaves us with one question: Has anyone checked Ronald Reagan's neck?

||||||||||||||||||||||||||||||||||||||||||||||||||||||||||

A CADILLAC RAN INTO A CAR ON PALOS VERDES DRIVE.

When the driver got out rubbing her neck, the Cadillac driver—instead of exchanging telephone numbers or insurance information—gave the driver a neck rub.

||||||||||||||||||||||||||||||||||||||||||||||||||||||||||

ACCORDING TO THE JOURNAL *OBSTETRICS AND GYNECOL-*

ogy, researchers at the University of Southern California School of Medicine conducted a study on estrogen replacement for postmenopausal women. Forget help for night sweats, hot flashes, and mood swings, what's important is the fact that women who were treated with estrogen scored higher on "income management."

||||||||||||||||||||||||||||||||||||||||||||||||||||||||

FROM THE *LOS ANGELES TIMES*, FIVE PERFECTLY GOOD
reasons to call 911:

1. Eighteen-year-old male can't get any rest at home, wants ride to hospital.
2. Thirteen-year-old stubbed her toe on a stereo speaker.
3. Person answered "no" to question, "Are you conscious?"
4. Lady has blisters from working three days at Taco Bell.
5. Out of breath from "running from police."

||||||||||||||||||||||||||||||||||||||||||||||||||||||||

ANNUAL COST OF CALIFORNIA LIABILITY INSURANCE FOR
yoga teachers with no employees: $299.00

||||||||||||||||||||||||||||||||||||||||||||||||||||||||

ACCORDING TO THE *GUINNESS BOOK OF WORLD RECORDS*,
the drunkest person on record was a twenty-four-year-old woman who was admitted to the UCLA Medical Center in 1982. A blood alcohol level of .40 is considered fatal; hers was 1.8.

ACCORDING TO A NEW AGE NEWSLETTER, SANTA BAR-

bara ranks number one for high colonics in the U.S. In Hope Ranch and Montecito, high colonics vans make monthly house calls.

NO, YOU SIT ON IT. ONE OF THE MAJOR CAUSES OF BAD

health, one West L.A. company claims, is a dense aura that blocks your *chi*, leaving you a physical wreck. Fear not, all you need is a 24-karat gold, copper, and Fiberglas disk—a "cosmic tuning fork," if you will. For "basic aura activation," carry the disk around in your pocket. To activate a beam of "harmonized energy," tape two disks to your walls. To enhance creativity, sit on it.

A CANOGA PARK COMPANY BELIEVES THAT SUPER BLUE-

green algae is "our natural defense in today's world." According to their literature, if you scarf down this stuff you will have "increased stamina, mental clarity, balanced mood swings [I believe this qualifies as an oxymoron], decreased cravings for sweets, and heightened immune functions." Before you start scraping the sides of your fish tank, take note: only blue-green algae "harvested wild from an unpolluted, pristine [isn't that redundant?], snow-fed Oregon lake"! will do the trick. One thing blue-green algae obviously won't do: improve your copy-writing skills.

|||||||||||||||||||||||||||||||||||||||||||||||||||||||||||

PREDICTION: EXPECT SIMPLER HAIRSTYLES AND FEWER

hard-to-hold curls. In order to clear the air, California's Air Resource Board has attacked hairspray, a notorious smog former. According to the law, in 1993 hairsprays must consist of a maximum of 80 percent hydrocarbons (usually butane or propane) and alcohol. That figure must drop to 55 percent by 1998.

|||||||||||||||||||||||||||||||||||||||||||||||||||||||||||

ACCORDING TO A *TIME* MAGAZINE POLL:

▌ Percentage of Californians who see themselves as health-conscious: 66%
▌ Percentage who see themselves as self-indulgent: 58%
▌ Percentage who see themselves as open-minded: 57%
▌ Percentage who see themselves as old-fashioned: 3%

||||||||||||||||||||||||||||||||||||||||||||||||||||||

IN 1992, THE SANTA CRUZ CITY COUNCIL APPROVED AN

ordinance that prohibited housing and employment discrimination based on looks. Nicknamed the "ugly ordinance," it is designed to protect "transgendered individuals" and forbids unequal treatment based on "sex, gender, sexual orientation, height, weight, or personal appearance." The sponsor of the bill, Neal Coonerty, said the legislation was inspired by a group called the Body Image Task Force.

||||||||||||||||||||||||||||||||||||||||||||||||||||||

IN A RELATED CASE, A WOMAN BELLHOP IN SAN FRAN-

cisco was ordered by management to shave her facial hair. The woman refused, saying that the hair, which included her mustache, was important to her sense of self.

||||||||||||||||||||||||||||||||||||||||||||||||||||||

IT WASN'T THE CHILD ABUSE, OR INSANITY, OR THE

adultery, in *The Prince of Tides* that bothered California moviegoers, it was Barbra Streisand's outdated nails. The trend was short and natural; she wore them long and red. *Los Angeles Times* editors were so upset by Ms. Streisand's manicure that they asked psychiatrists to explain why this woman could so horribly sabotage her film. According to one, "she distracts audiences from her nose" by calling attention to her hands.

LOST IN SPACE

MY COUSIN RACHEL FROM MARIN COUNTY JUST GRADU-

ated from the Universal School of Aura Maintenance. (She's planning to open her own garage.) Since I was invited to the postgraduation party, I thought I should bring a gift. Somehow I knew (was it ESP?) that luggage would not be appropriate, so I toddled on down to the New Age Bookstore.

The sign out front said: TOOLS FOR ENLIGHTENMENT, GENTLE SOULS WELCOME. I braced myself and opened the door. Just as I expected, I was nearly driven to my knees by the onslaught of patchouli incense, which immediately shut off my nasal passages and left me gasping for oxygen.

The smell of patchouli also dredges up memories I would prefer to leave nestled in my subconscious, where they undermine my efforts to establish loving relationships and set realistic career goals but do not remind me of the afternoon I spent in someone's basement giggling and listening to Frank Zappa while I watched my friends hyperventilate until they passed out. (We had flipped a coin and I was the one chosen to remain conscious—a 1960s version of the designated driver.)

A woman behind the counter whose skirt looked like it was made out of a chenille bedspread with most of the chenilles missing smiled beatifically but left me alone. One glance around the store and my gentle soul was overwhelmed by the array of merchandise. There may be one truth, but there are many tapes and videos (MasterCard and Visa accepted).

"I don't know where to start," I said to myself, but the woman in the bedspread overheard and asked, "Should I divine your intention through a tarot reading?" I wasn't sure what she meant, so I shook my head no, grabbed a "Cosmic Egg," and studied it as if it held the meaning of the Universe, which it may for all I know. The accompanying brochure told me that this egg was a chakra opener. I believe cousin Rachel's chakras are dilated a full ten centimeters; anything more would be vulgar.

Next I turned to a guide on astral projection. I have a few questions about this astral travel stuff. If I can be in two places at one time, will one of me be naked? Or does astral travel require a separate wardrobe? And if I can be in two places at one time, can one of them be Maui? Or do I have to accumulate frequent flyer points first? I closed the book; it wouldn't do. If astral projection is possible, I'm sure Rachel, whose reality fuse blew when I told her there was no Santa Claus, had already mastered it.

In quick succession I ruled out an Australian didjeridoo (hollowed out by ants), a set of rune stones, a set of ceremonial smudge sticks, 14-karat gold pentacles, a device that eliminates electromagnetic pollution from quartz watches, goddess earrings, and an orbital space calendar.

Last year, Rachel told me that she had to rent storage space for her spiritual quest accoutrements. What, I asked myself, do you give a New Age junkie?

Then it dawned on me (divine intervention?). You give 'em a break. A few seconds of unconsciousness may do Rachel a world of good. I know I've still got the Zappa album. If I can just remember how many rapid breaths it takes before you pass out.

ACCORDING TO *TIME* MAGAZINE, SYLVESTER STALLONE

believes he was beheaded during the French Revolution. In true Rambo fashion, Stallone claims he felt no pain, only the sensation of his head hitting the basket.

IN ARCATA, YOU CAN FIND THE ORIGINAL KLEPTONIAN

Neo-American Church of California, where Robert Funk is the Boo-Hoo General.

||||||||||||||||||||||||||||||||||||||||||||||||||||||||

THE LATE YUL BRYNNER HAD HIS PET SHAR-PEI'S MIND

read by a psychic. Communicating telepathically, the dog told her that traveling and pine household cleaner made his stomach hurt.

||||||||||||||||||||||||||||||||||||||||||||||||||||||||

A CALIFORNIA STUDY: "I WOULD LIKE TO HEAR FROM

anyone with a paranormal experience that could be taken as evidence of the survival of animals beyond death (i.e. seeing a ghost of the animal, seeing one in a near-death experience or during what is commonly referred to as astral projection)."

||||||||||||||||||||||||||||||||||||||||||||||||||||||||

SECRET SAUCER BASE EXPEDITIONS, A GROUP OF L.A. UFO

watchers, makes regular trips to Rachel, Nevada, an area they claim is excellent for spotting extraterrestrial flying machines. The California saucer watchers had such a positive impact on Rachel's economy, the owners of the local diner renamed their restaurant The Little A'Le'Inn.

||||||||||||||||||||||||||||||||||||||||||||||||||||||||||

FEELING TIRED AND STUPID? PAY MORE ATTENTION TO

your fingernails. According to the Esalen Institute at Big Sur, energy and wisdom flow through your cuticles.

||||||||||||||||||||||||||||||||||||||||||||||||||||||||||

A MEDIUM TOLD ACTRESS ANN FRANCIS THAT HER DOG

had been a despicable human in a former life and that Francis's adopted daughter was from Venus.

||||||||||||||||||||||||||||||||||||||||||||||||||||||||||

MIKE YACONELLI, A CHRISTIAN MINISTER WHOSE CHURCH

is in Yreka, also edits a satirical religious magazine called *The Door*. Readers are treated to regular features such as "Dogs Who Know the Lord" and news flashes like "Bigfoot Professes Christ at Billy Graham Crusade." Cartoons have included a chainsaw-carrying minister wearing a hockey mask, and a drawing of Jesus spying on a couple in bed.

||||||||||||||||||||||||||||||||||||||||||||||||||||||

INTERFERENCE? AT A SAN FRANCISCO 49ERS GAME, JACOB

Atabet claims he saw a two-story-tall flaming angel. Atabet says the angel flew across the field just as the running back caught a pass and made his way to the end zone for a touchdown.

||||||||||||||||||||||||||||||||||||||||||||||||||||||||

THE MEANING OF LIFE ACCORDING TO "ONE OF THE

Earth's Few Living Masters," who operates out of Fairfax: "There is only one truth. It is being where you are. And where you are is where your body is." Thanks for the tip.

||||||||||||||||||||||||||||||||||||||||||||||||||||||

ARTIST JOSE ANTONIO BURCIAGA HAD GREAT PLANS FOR

a mural at Stanford's Chicano-theme eating hall. He wanted to depict the Last Supper with Christ and the twelve disciples eating tortillas and tamales instead of bread, and drinking tequila instead of wine. The idea was nixed by the students.

||||||||||||||||||||||||||||||||||||||||||||||||||||

THE GANDHI MEMORIAL FOUNDATION IN SAN FRANCISCO

wanted to give Santa Monica a present: a fourteen-foot statue of Mohandas K. Gandhi, the great Hindu leader who devoted his life to nonviolent social reform. The Santa Monica City Council said "Yes, thank you" and wanted to put the statue at Palisades Park.

The Santa Monica Historical Society, however, acted very un-Gandhi-like. Members of the society said the statue had nothing to do with Santa Monica and was not welcome in the park. If thwarted, they threatened to take their fight to the Coastal Commission, which has the last word in deciding these matters. Gandhi's grandson was surprised at the furor caused by the gift, saying that his grandfather's philosophy was universal and that it need not be related to a particular city.

JOE NEVOTTI WAS AN EX-MARINE, A PH.D., AND A SUC-

cessful management consultant in San Francisco. He had a sailboat, a bay-view apartment, and a live-in girlfriend. He also had hair. Joe gave it all up in 1992 when he became a Buddhist monk—only the third American in twenty years to do so. How did he let his girlfriend know about his decision to give up his worldly goods? He called her on his car phone.

FROM *BEVERLY HILLS* [213]: "ASTROLOGER KARON

Christian is so good she lost her secretary! She told her which day to buy a lottery ticket. Her secretary did and won, then the unloyal girl quit!" (I guess everything in Beverly Hills rates an exclamation point.)

ACCORDING TO ONE PERSONAL GROWTH TRAINING CEN-

ter in Mill Valley, seminar participants can achieve personal growth by breathing rapidly, listening to drumming music, and drawing mandalas. As a group leader explains, these activities enable you to relive your birth, your grandfather's birth, a complete stranger's birth, or your birth during a past life. (Why, I wonder, would you want to relive *anyone's* birth?)

||||||||||||||||||||||||||||||||||||||||||||||||||||||||||||

AT THE SAN FRANCISCO NEW AGE FAIR, DAVID HOWIE, A

geomancer, offered a special on his specialty: reading your home's spiritual energy to determine if you share your space with an angel or other not-so-benign spirits. Our question is, if you are sharing your space, can you make the spirits kick in their share of the rent?

||||||||||||||||||||||||||||||||||||||||||||||||||||||||||||

ACCORDING TO DICK BERNAL, PASTOR OF THE JUBILEE

Christian Church Center in San Jose, California is in a mess of trouble. Bernal and his 5,500 church members are waging war with the spirits who trouble the state. Bernal believes that San Francisco is dominated by the Spirit of Perversion, Oakland by Murder, and San Jose by Greed. Worse yet, Marin County is held in thrall by the New Age Spirit. "Ever since the Gold Rush," Bernal said, "the free-thinking Spirit of Self has been holding sway over Northern California." He goes on to explain that the Spirit is an "independent, haughty spirit that encourages people to join the New Age movement."

||||||||||||||||||||||||||||||||||||||||||||||||||||||||||||

IN LOS ANGELES THEY HAVE THEIR OWN VERSION OF THE

Nativity procession in which Mary and Joseph are illegal aliens who have just entered the country from Tijuana. When they go to the homeless shelter, there is no room. Mary and Joseph are hassled by street vendors who threaten to turn them in to Immigration. Finally, after Mary crumples in a heap on the sidewalk, street gangs step in to help deliver the baby Jesus.

||||||||||||||||||||||||||||||||||||||||||||||||||||||

CLAIRVOYANTS, PALM READERS, TAROT CARD READERS,

and others who predict the future must be licensed in Los Angeles. The initial fee in 1991 was $450, with an annual renewal fee of $100. Astrologer Larry Pines predicted, "People are going to complain about it."

||||||||||||||||||||||||||||||||||||||||||||||||||||||

AFTER HE WAS HOSPITALIZED IN 1988, CARROLL

Righter, astrologer to the stars, including Marlene Dietrich, Joan Fontaine, and Princess Grace, predicted that he would not survive his hospital stay. He was correct and died at age eighty-eight.

||||||||||||||||||||||||||||||||||||||||||||||||||||||

SAINT ANDREWS CATHOLIC CHURCH IN OAKLAND SPENT

$11,000 for a fence to keep prostitutes off church property. The pastor and his ninety-two-year-old mother were tired of finding stockings, underwear, used condoms, and copulating couples on the rectory stairs.

||||||||||||||||||||||||||||||||||||||||||||||||||||||||||||

A TWAIN HARTE MAN SUED AND WON AN OUT-OF-COURT

settlement after he attended a California human potential seminar. The program, he claimed, left him "dreaming in a waking state." In the suit James Haslip said that participants went without food and sleep, were asked to imagine tragic situations such as the deaths of their loved ones, and were told to recall on paper each unhappy moment of their lives. After he left the seminar, Haslip lost control of his car and crashed. He had enrolled hoping to learn better sales techniques.

||||||||||||||||||||||||||||||||||||||||||||||||||||||||||||

RODEO DRIVE ART DEALER JACK PURSEL MOONLIGHTS AS

a channeler for the spirit of Lazaris. Pursel, who numbers among his "friends" Ted Danson, Andy Williams, and Barry Manilow, charges about $700 and warns that not all mediums are on the up-and-up. He says, "There's some loony tunes out there."

||||||||||||||||||||||||||||||||||||||||||||||||||||||||||||

BEVERLY HILLS RESIDENT MARY ELLEN TRACY, ALSO

known as Sabrina Aset, was arrested for prostitution. As part of her defense, she claimed to be a high priestess of an ancient cult that included sexual rituals as part of the worship service. Acolytes left offerings, which happened to include money. The court didn't buy it. Tracy was sentenced to one year in prison.

||||||||||||||||||||||||||||||||||||||||||||||||||

BEFORE HIS ORDINATION AS A ROMAN CATHOLIC CARDI-

nal, Bishop Roger M. Mahoney dodged the L.A. traffic problem by zipping around in his $400,000 jet helicopter. When he assumed his new duties, Cardinal Mahoney sold the helicopter, claiming that his schedule would prohibit him from keeping up with new aviation regulations.

||||||||||||||||||||||||||||||||||||||||||||||||||

ACCORDING TO *PARADE* MAGAZINE, JON ERIK BECKJORD

of the Crypto-Phenomena Museum in Malibu makes it his business to examine NASA satellite photos. In photographs of Mars he has found the image of Tammy Faye Bakker, complete with mile-and-a-half long eyelashes, and the countenance of Senator Edward Kennedy. Beckjord explains, "Of course, you could say this is not actually Teddy Kennedy; you could say it's something that *looks* like Teddy Kennedy. It's a volcano, the crater of which gives the impression of a square face with jowls, fat jowls, a chin protruding out of the jowls. He's got similar eyes, you can see an eyebrow and a lock of hair coming down over the head, and there's a slight smirk on the face. All of this, of course, is lava." When he was informed of Beckjord's findings, Kennedy said, "I knew I should have stopped eating those Mars bars."

||||||||||||||||||||||||||||||||||||||||||||||||||||

ACCORDING TO A *SAN FRANCISCO CHRONICLE* POLL:

24% of Bay Area residents believe in reincarnation and astrology.
38% believe people can have contact with spirits of the dead.
35% practice some type of meditation or yoga at least once a week.
57% believe Mother Earth has a consciousness of her own.
26% believe Satan or demonic power is at work behind the New Age movement.

||||||||||||||||||||||||||||||||||||||||||||||||||||

ELIZABETH CLAIRE PROPHET, LEADER OF THE CHURCH

Universal and Triumphant, believes that she is the reincarnation of Marie Antoinette and King Arthur's Guinevere. The church was founded in California but moved to Montana, a better location to sit out the impending nuclear holocaust that Ms. Prophet has predicted.

||||||||||||||||||||||||||||||||||||||||||||||||||||

MEMBERS OF THE CHURCH OF THE DIVINE LIGHT WERE

granted fire permits by San Francisco authorities so that group members who wanted to rid themselves of their worldly goods could toss them into a huge bonfire.

||||||||||||||||||||||||||||||||||||||||||||||||||||

THE CURRENT (1993) GURU OF CHOICE IS A FORMER

nightclub singer from Texas, Marianne Williamson. She preaches about love and miracles and draws support from Hollywood celebs like Oprah Winfrey, Barbra Streisand, and Cher. Williamson confirmed her status when she officiated at Elizabeth Taylor's most recent wedding (at this printing, to Larry Fortensky). According to her detractors, however, Williamson charges $7 a head for church attendance and her temper has alienated some supporters. Williamson admits she may be "the bitch for God."

||||||||||||||||||||||||||||||||||||||||||||||||||||

SECTION 43.30 OF THE LOS ANGELES MUNICIPAL CODE

(1944) reads:

Fortune Telling: No person shall advertise by sign, circular, handbill, or in any newspaper, periodical or magazine, or other publication or publications, or by any other means, to tell fortunes, to find or restore lost or stolen property, to locate oil wells, gold or silver or other ore or metal or natural product; to restore lost love or friendship or affection, to unite or procure lovers, for or without pay, by means of occult or psychic powers, faculties or forces, clairvoyance, psychology, psychometry, spirits, mediumship, seership, prophecy, astrology, palmistry, necromancy, or other craft, science, cards, talismen, charms, potions, magnetism or magnetized articles or substances, oriental mysteries or magic of any kind or nature, or numerology, or to engage in or carry on any business the advertisement of which is prohibited by this section. [That should about cover it. Obviously, the law no longer stands. Pity.]

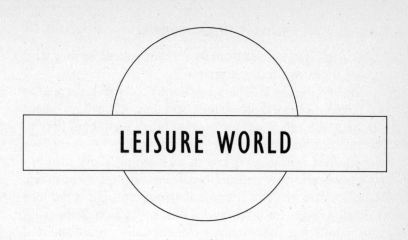

LEISURE WORLD

||||||||||||||||||||||||||||||||||||||||||||||||||||||||||||||||

CALIFORNIA COULD BE CALLED "THE THEME PARK
State." (It could also be called "The Land of Lunacy," but it
might take offense.) California has Disneyland, Knott's Berry
Farm, Michael Jackson's backyard, and, of course, Liz Taylor's
wedding, a major annual event that attracts thousands of tourists (many of them Liz's ex-husbands).

Californians, however, loathe theme parks, and they cannot endure the idea of attending another wedding in which
Liz, dressed in off-off-white, promises to love and cherish some
poor devil until death do they part or until the ink dries
on the marriage certificate—whichever comes first. Actually,
Californians do not particularly like to mingle with non-

Californians (i.e., people from their home states), so they have devised their own little pastimes.

There's the aforementioned Gumby collecting, there's the beach, there's drive-by shootings, and there's bowling. Pshaw, you say, Californians are too cool to bowl. Well, I am here to tell you (not that you asked), "You are wrong."

The fact is, California has more bowling alleys than any other state. This may explain in part the earthquake problem. Geologists theorize that the simultaneous crashing of millions of bowling balls into billions of pins at 7:42 on Wednesday nights could precipitate a major tremor. Californians, addicted as they are to excitement, laugh in the face of danger and lace up those very attractive green and red shoes that have been worn by at least 631,000 people before them.

If bowling is so popular, you might ask, why has Hollywood not made a bowling movie? Once again, I am here to tell you, "Hollywood has." Almost. It was called *Lane of Dreams*, a story about a young man who hears a voice telling him, "If you build it, he will come." The "it," of course, is a bowling alley. The sad truth is that once Kevin Costner was signed to do the film, it was discovered that, although he has a very nice butt, he cannot bowl worth a darn. The studio tried stand-ins, but Mr. Costner balked. It was very difficult to get into the role, to portray the intense inner life of a bowler, without actually bowling. Thus, that baseball movie. (Mr. Costner can *catch* a ball, he just can't roll them very well.)

The whispering around Hollywood these days is that Tom Cruise feels he is ready to do a bowling movie. Tom, who spent his honeymoon with Nicole at Frank's Leisure Lanes in Garden Grove, is quite a good bowler (and has a cute butt).

Everyone in Hollywood is dying to see the script, to be a part of cinematic history. Our diligent sleuthing has turned up a copy. Here, for the first time anywhere, is a brief synopsis of the film:

Tom plays the son of a professional bowler who was disgraced. In an effort to clear his father's name, Tom enters the bowling academy where, against ruthless competition, he must prove himself worthy. Trouble begins when Tom is distracted by his love for the shoecheck girl (played by Nicole Kidman). In a stunning finale, with an action sequence the likes of which Hollywood has never seen, Tom's manhood and honor are forged upon the crucible of the lanes.

Here we will leave you, not wanting to spoil the ending. You will have to wait with the rest of America to learn the outcome. Buck up—in the meantime you can look forward to Liz's next wedding.

JULY 4TH: IT BRINGS TO MIND HOT DOGS, PARADES, THE

American flag, and fireworks. A nineteen-year-old Reseda man thought he'd ring in the Fourth with a bang and blew his hand off after he lit a stick of dynamite. Residents within a two-block radius of the young man's home were evacuated while the bomb squad searched for and found his cache of explosives, hidden in his parents' garage.

DOUG PECK IS THE FATHER OF CENTIPEDE RACING. THE

idea came to him, he said, while he and a friend were running through a field of tomato plants. (Why they were running through a field of tomato plants is anybody's guess.) The two men seized a piece of plastic, cut holes in it, and got some friends to join them. They stuck their heads through the holes, attached styrofoam balls to wire, then entered their rig in the Bay to Breakers Road Race. The idea caught on, and now other groups run as six-packs of beer, lobsters, yachts, and land sharks.

‖‖

ACCORDING TO ACCORDION HISTORIANS, THE PIANO AC-

cordion was invented in San Francisco around 1907 by Colombo Piatanesi of North Beach. In recognition of this momentous event, Tom Torriglia and other aficionados wanted the San Francisco Board of Supervisors to officially recognize the instrument. Fifty accordionists gathered at City Hall to play "Lady of Spain." They gained the support of Supervisor Willie Kennedy, who said, "I'm only introducing an accordion resolution, but I want hearings on it. The issue will go to committee, but I intend that it not get stalled there. We need to act on it."

‖‖

THE BEVERLY HILTON WAS THE SITE OF THE 1991 FLORAL

Headdress Ball. Over eight hundred attendees applauded the flowery headdresses, which were inspired by movies such as *Camelot* and *Gigi*. (May we respectfully suggest that these folks get a life?)

DOLORES STREET IN SAN FRANCISCO IS THE SITE OF THE

Marijuana Festival. Here revelers, who are told to "BYOM," hark back to the 1960s and smoke pot publicly without police intervention. They also sing the praises of hemp. According to festival goers, the first drafts of the Constitution were written on hemp paper and Henry Ford used the plant to develop methanol for his cars.

THE ROSICRUCIAN EGYPTIAN MUSEUM IN SAN JOSE HAS

more mummies than any other West Coast museum. One mummy, Usermontu, dead since 630 B.C. and purchased from Neiman-Marcus, is displayed with his tongue sticking out.

A SAN DIEGO ENTREPRENEUR NICKNAMED CAPTAIN

Sticky organizes "real-men" tours. One adventure called the "Real Man's Mid-Life Crisis Tour of Thailand" includes plenty of bar- and brothel-hopping. Highlight of the two-week tour is a visit to the Kangaroo Bar, which is billed as "one of the world's five sleaziest bars."

THE NOW-DEFUNCT HOLYLAND IN MT. WASHINGTON WAS

once the home of a 1400-pound Fiberglas, steel, and birdseed bust of Elvis. The head was originally Mississippi's entry in the Rose Bowl parade. It was towed back to its home state after making a stop at Graceland but the Elvis head did not return to glory. It ended up in a junkyard. Holyland's owners heard of the head's plight and, for a modest sum, recovered the bust. In celebration of its return and in honor of Elvis's birthday, visitors to Holyland were offered pieces of bacon—Elvis's favorite food.

|||||||||||||||||||||||||||||||||||||||||||||||||||

ACCORDING TO A SPOKESPERSON FOR THE RICHARD

Nixon Library and Birthplace in Yorba Linda, the gift shop's bestseller is a photograph of Tricky Dick shaking hands with Elvis Presley. In order to satisfy all your disgraced president needs, the photo is also reproduced on pins, postcards, and refrigerator magnets.

|||||||||||||||||||||||||||||||||||||||||||||||||||||

THE WORLD'S SHORTEST WALK OF FAME IS THE COUNTRY

Music Walk of Fame on Lankersheim Street in Los Angeles. There, a lone star honors Eddie Rabbitt. Plans for expansion were squashed over ten years ago when the owner and City Hall began squabbling over permits.

|||||||||||||||||||||||||||||||||||||||||||||||||||||

WHILE YOU'RE TRAVELING IN CALIFORNIA, HERE ARE A

few attractions bound to be of interest to the whole family:

- The Sun Maid Raisin Tour, Fresno
- English Brass Rubbing Center, Inglewood
- Wooz Maze, Vacaville
- Skirball Museum, L.A.
- Petaluma Cheese Factory
- Skunk Railroad, Fort Bragg

- Barbie Doll Hall of Fame, Palo Alto
- Confusion Hill, Piercy (we thought this was in the District of Columbia)
- Ecological Staircase, Mendocino
- Moe's Doll Museum, San Francisco
- Herman's House of Guns, Siskiyou County
- Chevron World of Oil Museum, San Francisco
- Federal Reserve World of Economics, San Francisco
- Tattoo Art Museum, San Francisco
- Museum of Dentistry (always a favorite with the kids), Orange County

IN 1965, WHEN UC-IRVINE STUDENTS VOTED ON A MAS-

cot, the anteater won. Opponents claimed that the voting was rigged. Nonetheless, the anteater, based on Johnny Hart's comic strip "B.C.," remains. "Zot!" is the school cry and Zeta Omega Tau the fraternity of choice. The only mascot stranger than UC-Irvine's is UC-Santa Cruz's banana slug—origin unknown.

USC OFFERS A COURSE IN GARBALOGY—THE STUDY OF

personal garbage—called Modern Material Culture Studies.

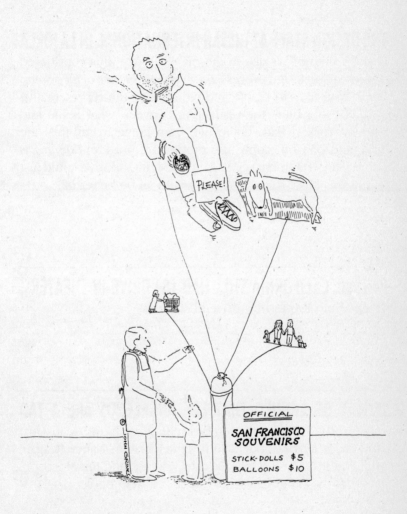

||||||||||||||||||||||||||||||||||||||||||||||||||||||

THE DESIGN STAFF AT NISSAN INTERNATIONAL IN LA JOLLA

is given time off to take in the movies. Two films considered critical to the design process: *Batman* and *Silence of the Lambs*. Why? "You have to let life into work," a Nissan representative said. "Design blurs the distinction between what is life and what is work." Okay, California, I am going to say this one time, and one time only: the movies are not life. *Batman* is not real and Hannibal Lecter is not real. If California could just accept this basic truth, then we would all be better off.

||||||||||||||||||||||||||||||||||||||||||||||||||||||

IN 1988, CALIFORNIA STILL HAD 184 DRIVE-IN THEATERS,

12 percent of America's drive-in screens.

||||||||||||||||||||||||||||||||||||||||||||||||||||||

IT MAY BE ARGUED THAT LOS ANGELENOS ARE A TAD

self-absorbed. Five of the ten bestselling books in L.A. in April 1991 were by or about California celebrities: Nancy Reagan, Julia Phillips, Ali MacGraw, Mickey Rooney, and Jim Morrison. Three of the other bestsellers were self-help books.

WHO SAYS SOUTHERN CALIFORNIANS AREN'T INTELLEC-

tuals? The Los Angeles Central Library keeps back copies of the *Enquirer* for six months and subscribes to the *Star* and the *Weekly World News*.

FOR THE INSOMNIAC WITH A GARTER FETISH: FREDER-

ick's of Hollywood's Lingerie Museum is open twenty-four hours a day.

- Amount Californians spent on in-line skates (Rollerblades) in 1991: $60 million
- Cost of fine for skating on Venice bike path: $25
- Average number of in-line skate injuries seen at Santa Monica Hospital each weekend: 6

UCLA AWARDS THE STEVE LAWRENCE AND EYDIE GORME

Scholarship to a deserving student each year. Not to be outdone, Cal State Northridge administers the $25,000 Buckwheat Memorial Scholarship.

THE WORLD CHAMPION PILLOW FIGHTS ARE HELD AN-

nually at Warm Springs Park in Kenwood. An intense rivalry has sprung up between Santa Rosa and Sonoma, whose teams use wet pillows to knock each other off a pole that straddles the creek. According to organizers, the team with the longest legs usually wins.

SAN DIEGO CAMPAIGNED HEAVILY TO BE THE SITE OF LEGO

World—a theme park planned by the makers of kids' building blocks. Supporters expected over one million tourists to flock to the park, which should feature a Mt. Rushmore and Statue of Liberty built out of Legos. The park has not yet been built.

AN EMPLOYEE AT THE LA BREA TAR PITS GOT STUCK IN

the asphalt while trying to retrieve a traffic cone someone had tossed into a pit. As he struggled to free himself, he was observed by a man and his child. Instead of offering to help, the man looked at the child and said, "See, that's what happened to the dumb animals."

VENICE IS THE SITE OF THE "DOGROMAT"—A DO-IT-

yourself dogwash facility. For ten bucks you get washing space, a Dalmation-motif apron to protect your clothes, and blow dryers. The facility also offers doggy treats and 1960s rock music.

AT DODGER STADIUM, FANS THROW BEACHBALLS

around, hit other people on the head with them, and make a general nuisance of themselves. During their training, Dodger Stadium ushers learn how to chase, catch, and destroy the errant balls.

IN SAN LUIS OBISPO COUNTY, YOU WILL FIND MORRO

Bay, home of the Giant Chess Board. The chess pieces, which weigh around twenty pounds each, are constructed from redwood and stand about three feet high. In one game, each player will move about one thousand pounds.

||||||||||||||||||||||||||||||||||||||||||||||||||||

THIS IS WHAT HOLLYWOOD STARS DO ON THEIR DAYS

off: According to *Beverly Hills (213)*, the quintessential gossip rag, Clint Eastwood had a bum time in Aspen. The water pipes burst and Clint had no water for TWO DAYS! Thank God for the Jacuzzi, BH tells us, and adds that "Clint also kept lots of Evian on hand for brushing his teeth."

||||||||||||||||||||||||||||||||||||||||||||||||||||

THE SAME PUBLICATION ALSO LET US KNOW THAT DON

Henley and Don Johnson are p.o.'d because Jon Peters, their Aspen neighbor, uses "too much water, therefore taking it away from the rest of the community." Awww.

||||||||||||||||||||||||||||||||||||||||||||||||||||

CALIFORNIA'S EXTRACURRICULAR ACTIVITIES INCLUDE

these clubs and organizations:

Pasadena Roving Archers
California Dry Bean Advisory Board
Sacramento Skeptics Society
Gee How Oak Pin Association
California Curling Association
Granite Curling Club of L.A.
Natural Colored Wool Association

California Payphone Association
River Dippers
Sacramento Tall Club
Mythopoeic Society
Far Western Garage Door Association
Sadistics Motorcycle Club
Stentorians of Southern California
Dharma Realm Buddhist Association
Hollywood Star Trekkers
American Society of Dowsers

||||||||||||||||||||||||||||||||||||||||||||||||||||

THE PENTHOUSE AT SAN FRANCISCO'S FAIRMONT HOTEL

is one of America's most expensive hotel suites. For $5,000 a night, you get eight rooms, a library with four thousand volumes, 24-karat gold faucets, a lapis lazuli fireplace, and maid service.

||||||||||||||||||||||||||||||||||||||||||||||||||||

A *LOS ANGELES TIMES* ART REVIEW OF AN EXHIBIT OF

work by Robert Gero: "Although his minimalist-derived sculptures have almost no mass, they have the presence of ancient icons to mysterious alchemical rituals. Almost not there but strangely potent, they offer a low-tech version of inclusive, cyclical movement."

||||||||||||||||||||||||||||||||||||||||||||||||||||||||

YOU KNOW THOSE TELEPHONE CONVERSATIONS WHERE

the person goes on and on and all you get to say is "Yeah" and "Uh-huh" and they won't shut up long enough for you to tell them you gotta go so finally you either wet your pants, die from starvation, or break in and say, "Someone's at the door, or my dog is in labor, or my son just fell off the roof"? A Walnut Creek company has come up with a device to put an end to your misery. Audio Ally is a cassette that supplies background noises to substantiate your lies. There's ringing doorbell, baby crying, office sounds, and much, much more. Feeling a little guilty about lying? Don't. The end justifies, etc., because, as the Audio Ally brochure states, "You have just purchased the means to avoid unpleasant situations and maintain control over how you spend your time."

||||||||||||||||||||||||||||||||||||||||||||||||||||||||

CALIFORNIA-BASED SALES OF SKATEBOARDS AND ACCES-

sories: $125 million per year.

||||||||||||||||||||||||||||||||||||||||||||||||||||||||

AT A GAME AGAINST THE CHICAGO BULLS, SAN DIEGO'S

mascot, the Famous Chicken, got carried away. Bulls' cheerleader Kimberly Smith said that she was tackled and rolled on by the Chicken during one of her routines. As a result, her arm and jaw were broken. She is suing the Chicken for $1 million.

SEX, LOVE, MARRIAGE, DIVORCE,

AND ALL THINGS IN BETWEEN

IN CALIFORNIA MARRIAGES AREN'T MADE IN HEAVEN, they're scripted in Hollywood. So many Californians have seen so many movies that ideas of love, relationships, marriage, and happily ever after are seriously skewed. Here marriages are measured in nanoseconds. In at least one instance, the divorce proceedings lasted longer than the relationship.

Perhaps Californians lost hope when the marriage of Tiny Tim and Miss Vicky failed. Perhaps it is this lost hope that has left them embittered. If we were to rate Californians' sentimentality, it would be comparable, say, to that of sea kelp.

Take, for instance, the reaction to the Julia-Kiefer debacle some years back. It was not a young man's broken heart that concerned California. ("Hey, she gave him twenty-four hours' notice," one source was quoted as saying. "This is Hollywood. He could have found someone else and gone on with the wedding as planned.") No, the overriding concern was: What in the hell are the bridesmaids going to do with the $400-a-pair, custom-dyed Ferragamos?

This coldness toward romance is not only reserved for endings but is often manifested before marriage as well. Couples spend more time on the wording of their prenuptial agreements than they do on their wedding vows. "Love doesn't last forever," one bride told me, "but if you play your cards right, annuities can." It is rumored that the Spielberg-Irving settlement was so large, the lawyer's secretary developed carpal tunnel syndrome typing the zeroes.

For all this lack of sentimentality, however, most Californians are inexplicably desperate to find a mate. It seems they will stop at nothing: dating services, personal ads, computer networks, singles clubs, sandwich boards, arranged marriages, assault with a deadly weapon.

One woman was so hard up she fell in love with Hannibal Lecter. When she found out he was a fictional character, she took an overdose of SlimFast. As she was hauled away, she screamed, "I gained twenty pounds for that man! I GAVE UP SPANDEX! Now you tell me he doesn't exist!"

She'll get over it. Where there is life there is hope, and where there is hope there is love, and where there's love there's a lawyer, waiting to prepare your prenups.

"He's into Gupta Yoga, Bluegrass music, Scrambler motorcycling, organic gardening, electronic sculpture and snowmobiling. A real Renaissance man."

A NORTH HOLLYWOOD COUPLE SPENT OVER 100 HOURS

communicating by computer before they met and eventually married. The attraction: "I could feel his compassion through the computer."

|||||||||||||||||||||||||||||||||||||||||||||||||||||||||||

RON GRAENING FILMED HIS MARRIAGE PROPOSAL TO

Shelley Gillad and convinced the management of a Tarzana theater to run the proposal before the feature film. Gillad said yes; the audience cheered.

|||||||||||||||||||||||||||||||||||||||||||||||||||||||||||

FOR THEIR WEDDING A PASADENA COUPLE HAD PEACH,

apricot, and quince blossoms flown in from Oregon, a five-foot wedding cake delivered by refrigerated truck from Texas, and 550 yards of ivory silk shipped from India. The grooms-men, who only had to travel a short distance, barely made it to the wedding. They got stuck in the hotel elevator.

|||||||||||||||||||||||||||||||||||||||||||||||||||||||||||

OR DOES IT JUST FIZZLE OUT? THE *BAY AREA COMMUNITY*

Health & Drug Report advertises "Sex Packets" as an answer to AIDS. The packet contains a powder and a pill that subconsciously stimulate sexual pleasure. After three to five minutes, the experience supposedly ends in orgasm.

FROM THE PERSONALS:

▎ "SWF looking for yuppie who grew up as a hippie child and now wants to get back to nature. Must be willing to relocate to mountains and start herb farm."

▎ "Winner of Henry Kissinger look-a-like contest seeking extraordinary female, 25–31, who wouldn't be afraid of wearing a beehive."

▎ "SWF, 27, involved in dental profession would like to meet a *real* man, not opposed to pain, for exploratory session. I've got a bountiful supply of nitrous oxide and Novocain (if you must).

▎ "Let's share fruit!"

▎ "I'm into reptiles, painted-on jeans and leather. Also, butt paraphernalia."

▎ "Be full of energy with phone in 213, 818, 714, 310 [area codes]."

▎ "Have fun. Expand your vocabulary. Meet me for a friendly game of Scrabble."

IF YOU'VE UPSET YOUR SPOUSE OR PARTNER AND WANT

to make amends but hate those embarrassing apologies that chip at your self-esteem, fret no more. Apologies Accepted, a Hollywood-based operation, will say "I'm sorry" for you. Owner Loren Harris assures prospective clients that hiring an outsider to do your dirty work is not impersonal. "Apologies are specialized for each client," he said. "I always ask, 'OK, Joe, on a scale of one to ten, how mad is she?'"

||||||||||||||||||||||||||||||||||||||||||||||||||||||||||||

WHEN MULTI-GRAMMY WINNER BONNIE RAITT MARRIED

actor Michael O'Keefe, she wore an ivory wedding gown. The father of the bride, actor John Raitt, wore a dress kilt.

||||||||||||||||||||||||||||||||||||||||||||||||||||||||||||

LESLIE HAMILTON AND NEIL NATHANSON MET OVER

crossword puzzles at a cafe. When it came time to propose, Nathanson popped the question in a crossword puzzle published in the *San Francisco Examiner*. Over one million readers solved the puzzle, but only Leslie got the ring. Her response: "I said 'yes' right away and we didn't even finish the puzzle."

||||||||||||||||||||||||||||||||||||||||||||||||||||||||||||

F. KORBEL & BROS., CHAMPAGNE MAKERS IN GUERNE-

ville, have a "Director of Romance" on their staff.

IN A STUDY AT STANFORD UNIVERSITY, SCIENTISTS FED

an African folk medicine called yohimbine to rats. The drug, purported to be an aphrodisiac, doubled the frequency with which the rats had sex: forty-five times in fifteen minutes. When the research team turned to humans to determine yohimbine's effects, the project director said, "Not surprisingly, we have an ample number of volunteers."

ALTERNATIVE LIFESTYLES CALL FOR ALTERNATIVE WED-

ding gifts, and California's merchants are happy to oblige. The Bike Sport, a shop in Canoga Park, has a bridal registry where couples can set down their preference for bikes or pick out matching athletic wear.

AN ADVERTISING SLOGAN FOR A SANTA MONICA BANK:

"We handle more zeroes than a dating service."

LAURIE STEPHENS AND KEVIN BRADY WERE MARRIED IN

a lovely ceremony at "Art to the Bone," a tattoo parlor in Hollywood. Reasoning that rings can be removed but tattoos are forever, the couple stopped the ceremony at the point where rings are usually exchanged and had black bands tattooed on their fingers.

SAN FRANCISCO WAS THE FIRST MAJOR CITY IN THE

United States that allowed unmarried couples to register their relationships. For a $35 fee, couples can fill out a form to declare their emotional and financial dependence on each other.

A SAN FRANCISCO WOMAN GAVE BIRTH TO A BABY GIRL

on a sidewalk downtown during rush hour, picked up the newborn, and kept on walking. When police caught up with the woman, she told them she hadn't known she was pregnant.

||||||||||||||||||||||||||||||||||||||||||||||||||||||||

WHEN SAN FRANCISCO SUPERVISOR BILL MAHER WED

deputy state attorney general Kay Yu, they registered for wedding gifts as any couple does, but not at the local gift shop. Maher and Yu chose to register their wants at their local liquor store.

||||||||||||||||||||||||||||||||||||||||||||||||||||||||

FOR YUPPIE COUPLES WHO WANT TO GIVE THEIR BABY

every advantage, there's Infant Advantage. Priced at around $1300, the cradle has a recording of blood rushing through the placenta, a built-in woofer, and mimics the walking motion of a pregnant woman.

||||||||||||||||||||||||||||||||||||||||||||||||||||||||

A MARRIAGE WITH ONE FOOT IN THE GRAVE: RONALD

Reagan and Jane Wyman were married at Forest Lawn Glendale (yes, the cemetery) on January 26, 1940.

||||||||||||||||||||||||||||||||||||||||||||||||||||||||

FOLLOWING THE "I DO" THERE IS USUALLY THE "LET'S

eat!" What began as a wedding reception at a restaurant in Monrovia turned into a parking lot free-for-all. For unspecified reasons, the formally clad guests began duking it out. It took twenty-five sheriff's deputies and reinforcements from the Monrovia and Arcadia police departments to subdue the crowd. Six people were arrested.

||||||||||||||||||||||||||||||||||||||||||||||||||||||||||||||||

IF YOU WANT TO TEST YOUR PARTNER'S SENSE OF HUMOR,

shop at CONDOMania on Melrose Avenue in Los Angeles, where you can buy glow-in-the-dark condoms and condoms shaped like Stealth Bombers.

||||||||||||||||||||||||||||||||||||||||||||||||||||||||||||||||

IN AN EFFORT TO PROMOTE CONDOM USE IN SAN FRAN-

cisco, the AIDS Foundation developed the "Rubberman" campaign, which included billboards, ads, and a pinup calendar. One billboard featured a handsome young man reclining amid the sheets wearing a come-hither look and little else. The caption read: "The Man of My Dreams is a Rubberman." The campaign also included a dozen or more rubbermen who worked the bars handing out free condoms.

||||||||||||||||||||||||||||||||||||||||||||||||||||||||||||||||

TAKE MY MOTHER-IN-LAW. PLEASE. ELIZABETH DUNCAN

had a hard time loosening those apron strings. After her son married, she tried to have the marriage annulled by posing in

♪ ♪ ♪

"RING AROUND THE WALLET,
RING AROUND THE WALLET "

SO
TACKY!

WHY SUFFER THE
EMBARRASSMENT OF
UNSIGHTLY "RUBBER-RING?"

JUST LOOK AT HOW HAMBLY'S NEW
"CONDOMIZER"™ BILLFOLD HIDES
YOUR LITTLE FRIEND:

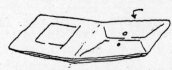

SO
CHIC!

ALSO AVAILABLE: "CONDOMIZER"™ BRIEFCASES,
PURSES & STEAMER TRUNKS FOR YOU HEAVY USERS!

court as her daughter-in-law. When that didn't work, Duncan was seriously upset. She hired two hitmen to murder her daughter-in-law. Duncan's son had no hard feelings, though, and spoke up in mom's defense during the murder trial.

A FREMONT COUPLE MARRIED IN A HOT TUB. THE HAPPY

couple wore traditional wedding garb—from the waist up—and the bride's nine-year-old daughter played Wagner's "Wedding March" on the harmonica.

HEADLINE: WOMAN REJECTS SUITOR, IS SERIOUSLY

wounded. A Downey woman was shot in the arm and side as she tried to slam the door on a suitor. The man had offered the woman perfume and had left flowers at her door twice in the week preceding the shooting. When questioned by police, she said that the man was a complete stranger.

AT THE NAPA WEDDING OF JAMES HJERBE AND COLETTE

Cufaude, the groom's Doberman pinscher was the ring bearer.

THE ORANGE COUNTY SUPERIOR COURT CLERK'S OFFICE

was drowning in paper, so the staff decided to clean out the divorce files. Over thirty thousand divorce cases dating back to 1984 were purged. During cleanup, however, it was discovered that 487 couples who thought they were long divorced were still legally married. They had failed to obtain a final judgment of dissolution of marriage. When he heard the news, a man who had married and divorced wives two and three while legally married to number one said he would gladly take his first wife back, but he wanted no part of wife number two.

DODDS BOOK SHOP IN L.A. OFFERS THIS SAGE ADVICE ON

its cash register receipts: "Practice Safe Sex . . . Take a Book to Bed."

A LETTER FOUND IN A BUSH IN GLENDALE MADE ITS WAY

to the *Los Angeles Times*. Columnist Jack Smith did not reveal the writer's identity and was kind enough to correct nearly all of her, as he described it, "atrocious" spelling. Here we have it, the end of romance:

"We now come to the point where we can really talk here, but I don't wish to make it hard. . . . I just want to express my feeling that I won't take this kind of carp [sic] any more.

"I really hate you, and think you are very sick, sick, sick, sick, sick, sick! Why do you keep doing the things you do? I really can't understand but I'll bet you have a real good reason. . . . I don't like it one bit.

"Maybe I will have to do something to you to make you stop pestering me with the clicking in my house. . . . I don't love you at all and can't think that you could be so crazy as to buy a house 200 yards from me."

WHEN A FOUR-YEAR RELATIONSHIP ENDED, PHILIPPE

Marcelis placed a personal ad in the *Los Angeles Times* classifieds: "Dining, Fireplace, Good food, 1 on 1, attr. prof. SW European M seeks prof. attr. SBF 25–35, slim, non-smkg." He got more, much more than he bargained for. Three days after his second date with a woman who had responded to the ad, Marcelis was attacked at his home. He was tied up, beaten, and robbed. According to Marcelis, his attacker aimed a pistol at him and pulled the trigger. The bullet barely missed him. After Marcelis reported the attack to the police, he began receiving threatening phone calls. The caller said he would kill Marcelis; he told him he would blow up his house. Following an investigation, police arrested a suspect. He was the friend of Marcelis's personal-ad dream girl.

MARIE AND JONATHAN FIRST MARRIED IN 1960, BUT AFTER

nineteen years of scrapping they filed for divorce. Before the final judgment of dissolution could be entered, however, they reconciled but decided to go on with the divorce to "clean out the emotional garbage." Then they would remarry. Marie moved to Oregon with Jonathan; six months later she moved back to California. Jonathan followed Marie to California, they reconciled, she moved back to Oregon. Three months later, in May, Marie moved out again. A month later she came back. Marie left again in August, they reconciled in February, and remarried in April. By August of the following year, Jonathan had found a woman willing to support him, to give him a Mercedes, and to pay for his divorce. This time Marie was history.

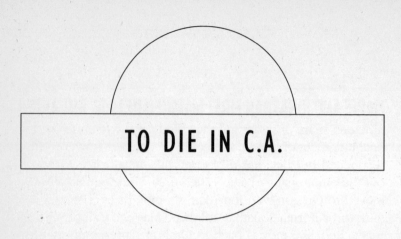

TO DIE IN C.A.

AS MUCH AS CALIFORNIANS LOVE TO RIDE IN LIMOU-
sines, there is one ride they are happy to pass up: the one to
the cemetery. In a state obsessed with perpetual youth, perpetual life, or a reasonable facsimile thereof, is the next logical
step. In the event that cryogenics fail, Californians have a fail-
safe plan: perpetual celebrity. A public relations firm in the
Midwest (a discreet distance away) now specializes in keeping
notable names in the news *ad infinitum*. I'm not famous and
I'm certainly not rich, but I wanna be, so I thought I'd give
the firm a call to see what services they offer.

"Good afternoon, Selby Management. We bring you out
of the twilight into the spotlight. How can I help you?"

"I'm a writer. I'm not famous yet, but I plan to be and I wondered if you could help me."

"One of our mottoes at Selby is, 'If you're still breathing, you don't need us.' Perhaps your people could contact us after you're gone."

"I don't have any 'people.' I have to make arrangements myself. Surely there's something I can do now to ensure I'm remembered after I die."

"Oh, please, not the D word. It sounds so *final*. Passed, transcended, departed. So much more civilized."

"Sorry. Can you help me?"

"Actually, now that you mention it, I can. Just recently we introduced our 'What a Way to Go' package. For $899.95 we offer a range of options to ensure that your passing is mentioned in the *L.A. Times*. For $1499.95 we guarantee that you'll make the evening news. Then, with your celebrity established, we build on it over the eons. We have several perpetual P.R. packages starting at . . ."

"Wait a minute. You said options. What exactly do you mean by options?"

"Options. Ways to die, I mean pass."

"For instance?"

"Okay. Take that poor guy who departed last week. Run down by a Dairy Darling skating waitress. That was no accident."

"You mean you arranged it?"

"Certainly. He was a real nobody, certain to be forgotten. But because of us, his passing was picked up by all the wire services, including Reuters. We have clippings from as far away as Hong Kong. Our next step is to get him into those tacky trade paperbacks that deal in bizarre events." (I let that one pass.)

"Then what can you do for me?"

"A writer, let me think. Scarf caught in laser printer? Paper cut infection—you'd make all the medical journals. Hand caught in electric pencil sharpener? Too grisly. Let me think, let me think. Oh, I've got it! We could arrange to have you erased."

"What? A hit man?"

"No, erased. Wiped out by a giant eraser. You'd be a smudge on the page of life, but you'd be remembered forever. Certain entry for Ripley's. Tabloids—front page. We have contacts. Oh, this is perfect. Let me get on it right away! Hello, hello, are you there? Oh, don't hang up."

I didn't hang up. I kept him on the line until I found every eraser in the house. I put them in a mayonnaise jar and sealed the lid. Surely without air they will die, sorry, I mean pass.

||||||||||||||||||||||||||||||||||||||||||||||||||||||||||||||||||

A HOMELESS MAN IN SACRAMENTO WAS PLACED AT DOR-

othy Puente's boarding house. After he disappeared, police began an investigation and found that Puente had a history of criminal behavior, including a prison term for misuse of board-and-care clients' funds. Alarmed police began digging in Puente's backyard. They found a body, but not the man they were looking for. Puente then asked investigators if she could visit her nephew at a hotel nearby. Not only was she granted permission, Puente was also escorted by a detective through police lines. Puente did not visit her "nephew," she disappeared. After seven bodies were found buried in her yard, a nationwide search was commenced and Puente's photograph was broadcast on TV. She was arrested the next day in Los

Angeles when an elderly man Puentes met in a bar grew suspicious when she began quizzing him about his Social Security benefits.

HAROLD C. "DUDE" SHERREL, ANAHEIM HILLS, DID NOT

die, his obituary noted, Dude merely "transcended into his new life."

IF YOU WERE TO VISIT HOLLYWOOD MEMORIAL PARK IN

search of Jayne Mansfield, the sex goddess who died in a violent auto accident, you would find a pink granite marker bearing the inscription "We live to love you more each day," but you wouldn't find Mansfield. The late actress is buried in Pennsylvania.

AFTER THE DEATH OF ACTOR JAMES MASON, HIS WIDOW

and children by a former marriage became embroiled in a nasty battle over the estate. In retaliation, Mason's widow refused for over seven years to tell the children where their father's remains were buried.

L.A. HAD A TOUGH TIME FINDING A COUNTY CORONER.

Their first pick turned down the job after his wife got a look at housing prices. The second choice, a former deputy New York City medical examiner, failed the California medical licensing test *three* times. A spokesman for the State Medical Board explained that the test is tough for pathologists because after med school, "they go right to corpses and don't deal with live people."

GROUNDSKEEPERS AT ROSE HILLS MEMORIAL PARK WERE

spooked when fires began flaming up in the trash receptacles at the cemetery. It was later discovered that Chinese families whose loved ones had been laid to rest at Rose Hills were following an ancient custom of burning paper money to help their dead relatives in the next world. After some consideration, Rose Hills officials began offering portable incinerators for the graves.

THE FACT THAT CALIFORNIA IS A MELTING POT CAN BEST

be illustrated by the funeral of Chinese businessman Ernest S. Wong, whose cortège was led by a New Orleans–style jazz band. Making its way through the streets of Chinatown, the procession moved back and forth, careful not to cross its path, in honor of the Chinese tradition but moving in tune to "When the Saints Come Marchin' In." The funeral had been arranged by Wah Wing Sang Gutierrez and Weber Mortuary.

||||||||||||||||||||||||||||||||||||||||||||||||||||||||||

TRADITIONALLY, CHINESE FUNERAL RITES REQUIRE mourners to leave a trail of paper along the procession route. The pieces of paper have holes cut in them to slow the journey of the serpent that follows the dead to the grave. While the serpent crawls through the small holes, the deceased is safely buried. This custom is no longer practiced in California, however. Litter laws.

||||||||||||||||||||||||||||||||||||||||||||||||||||||||||

SHOULD WE CALL THE ASPCA? PET HAVEN IN GARDENA is the burial site for celebrity pets. The late Michael Landon's horse from "Bonanza" is buried here, along with *sixteen* of Jerry Lewis's dogs.

||||||||||||||||||||||||||||||||||||||||||||||||||||||||||

A FORTY-TWO-YEAR-OLD WOMAN IN CHATSWORTH DIED after three calls to 911 failed to bring help. Family members were told the woman either had the flu, food poisoning, or was having an anxiety attack. The 911 operator suggested that she breathe into a paper bag. It didn't work. The woman was having a heart attack.

||||||||||||||||||||||||||||||||||||||||||||||||||||||||||||

REAL ESTATE MILLIONAIRE SEITA ONISHI OF JAPAN HAS

erected a $15,000 cenotaph, two tablets, and a bronze fallen sparrow at the site of James Dean's death in Cholome. Onishi commissioned a 120-ton, 36-inch tall limestone monument to be installed at the site in 1990, but the Hearst Corporation, which owns the land, refused permission for the placement of the monument.

||||||||||||||||||||||||||||||||||||||||||||||||||||||||||||

MONTHS IN WHICH CALIFORNIANS ARE MOST LIKELY TO

die: December and January.

||||||||||||||||||||||||||||||||||||||||||||||||||||||||||||

THE LAMB FUNERAL HOME IN PASADENA HAD A CORNER

on the cremation market. Their pickup service extended to the Mexican border, and for a mere $75 the deceased would be cremated and within a week their ashes returned. Officials later discovered that the funeral home would cremate as many as fifteen bodies at a time and portion out the intermingled remains to the families. At a subsequent trial, witnesses said that gold fillings were pried from corpses' teeth with a screw-driver, and that eyes and other vital organs were sold to scientific supply companies. The funeral home's owners made an estimated $5,000 a month from the gold fillings alone. When a tentative $15.4 million settlement was reached, the judge estimated that as many as twenty thousand families may be eligible to claim part of the money.

||||||||||||||||||||||||||||||||||||||||||||||||||||||||

PREVIOUSLY, ONE OF THE OWNERS OF THE ABOVE MEN-

tioned mortuary had been charged in the death of his chief competitor. Authorities accused him of poisoning his rival with oleander, an attractive but very deadly shrub. Charges were dropped, however, when tests showed no trace of the plant in the man's body.

||||||||||||||||||||||||||||||||||||||||||||||||||||||||

SOME FOLKS CALL IT PARADISE, BUT CALIFORNIA'S SUI-

cide rate is 16 percent higher than the national average.

||||||||||||||||||||||||||||||||||||||||||||||||||||||||

GALLOWS HUMOR:

| If the Show Fits. On the night before their executions at San Quentin, convicted murderers Jack Santo and Emmet

Perkins ate fried chicken and watched "You Bet Your Life."
The last songs Wilson De la Roi heard (at his request)
before his trip to the gas chamber were "I Want a Pardon
for Daddy" and "I'll Be Glad When You're Dead You Rascal
You." De la Roi also asked for a roll of antacids, joking
that he needed them for gas.

California's execution by hanging was replaced by the gas
chamber in 1938. The chamber's first victim was a pig.

A SUNNYDALE MATHEMATICIAN, THOMAS DONALDSON,

who suffered from a brain tumor petitioned the court to allow
him to have his head cryonically suspended—in other words,
flash frozen—*before* he died. Donaldson hoped to have his
head removed before the tumor had seriously damaged his
brain. The court turned down his petition.

COST OF CRYONICALLY FREEZING AND MAINTAINING A

head at the Alcor Life Extension Foundation in Riverside:
$35,000 (1990 price).

|||||||||||||||||||||||||||||||||||||||||||||||||||||||||

THE *SANTA CRUZ SENTINEL* OBITUARY OF NAN STOCKS-

dale, seventy-four, noted that she was a woman "who loved chocolate and was a member of the Shakespeare Club. At her request, no services will be held. She asked that those who wish to memorialize her eat chocolate instead."

|||||||||||||||||||||||||||||||||||||||||||||||||||||||||

DOUGLAS AND DANA RIDENOUR WERE FOUND DEAD IN

their home on August 1, 1990. According to the police, the couple died from shotgun blasts in what appeared to be a murder-suicide. It quickly became apparent that the two had been planning their deaths for months. They quit their prosperous real estate jobs in April, bought a twelve-gauge shotgun, paid for their cremation services in advance, and cancelled their newspaper subscription. The day of their deaths, they mailed a fifteen-minute video to Douglas's brother. In the video, the couple explained that "after twenty-two years of marital bliss, they dreaded growing old." Douglas was forty-eight; Dana was forty-five.

SAN FRANCISCO'S GHIA GALLERY SPECIALIZES IN FUNERAL

furnishings designed by artists. One casket rests on chicken feet, another is neon-painted plywood. For those with claustrophobia, Ghia Gallery offers glass urns for cremated ashes ("So you can look out").

ARE WE GOING FOR A RECORD HERE? LANCE THOMAS

sells expensive timepieces—Rolexes and antique pocket watches—which are very attractive to thieves. To protect his store, Thomas put the word out on the street: he had an arsenal of weapons and knew how to use them. Anybody trying to rob his store wouldn't get out alive. Thomas has made good on that promise. Since August 1989, he has shot and killed four robbers and wounded a fifth. A fifth man was killed in the store during an attempted holdup, but police were not certain whether Thomas or an employee fired the fatal shot. Each time, the LAPD ruled the killings justifiable.

HER FAMILY WATCHED AS HER CREMATED ASHES WERE

interred at Forest Lawn in Glendale. They were comforted by the idea that their loved one was at peace in the beautifully landscaped surroundings. The day after the interment, however, a Caltrans worker found a box used to transport ashes lying on the Glendale Freeway. The box, which bore the woman's name, had been hit by a car and about half of the ashes had scattered along the freeway and in the median. Forest Lawn officials were at a loss to explain what had happened or who had been interred the day before. The family is suing.

IN LOS ANGELES, GRAVELINE TOURS OFFERS VISITORS A

look at the dying grounds of the stars. Included on the tour, which is conducted from a hearse, are the sites of Freddie Prinze's and George Reeves's suicides, John Belushi's and Janis Joplin's overdoses, and Sal Mineo's murder. For fear of violating good taste, however, the tour does not enter star-studded cemeteries.

BELA LUGOSI, BEST KNOWN FOR HIS ROLE AS COUNT

Dracula, was buried in his vampire cape.

GRAVESTONE EPITAPHS:

"Bye, Guy"—Ted Knight, best known for his role as news anchor Ted Baxter on "The Mary Tyler Moore Show."

▌ "Go Away, I'm Asleep"—During her lifetime, actress Joan Hackett (*The Group*) so craved her rest that she often tacked this message to her door. Friends who had been turned away by this line thought it a most fitting epitaph.

▌ "Here in nature's arms I nestle, free at last from Georgie Jessel." —Eddie Cantor composed his own epitaph.

▌ "There comes a time in every man's life, and I've had plenty of them." —Baseball great Casey Stengel, known for his malapropisms.

▌ "Dear God,
Thanks.
Ed Wynn"

▌ "That's All, Folks!" —Mel Blanc

SOURCES

"All Things Considered,"
    National Public Radio
American Health
Architectural Digest
Associated Press
Beverly Hills [213]
California Almanac (Pacific
    Data Resources, 1991)
California magazine
California Reporter
Chattanooga Times
Christian Science Monitor

The City (San Francisco, CA)
Daily Breeze (Hermosa
    Beach, CA)
Daily Post-Athenian (Ath-
    ens, TN)
Esquire
*Guinness Book of World
    Records* (Bantam Books,
    1992)
Harper's
*Hermosa Beach Hometown
    News* (Hermosa Beach, CA)

High Times
Kingsport Times-News
   (Kingsport, TN)
Knoxville Journal
Knoxville News-Sentinel
L.A. Is the Capital of Kansas
   (Crown, 1988)
Los Angeles Times
M magazine
New Yorker
Newsweek
Obstetrics and Gynecology
Old Farmer's Almanac
Parade
People Weekly

Permanent Californians
   (Chelsea Green, 1989)
Sacramento Bee
San Diego Union
San Francisco Chronicle
San Francisco Examiner
*Southern California: Off the
   Beaten Path* (Globe Pe-
   quot Press, 1989)
Spirit Speaks
Time
TV Guide
United Press International
Wall Street Journal
Washington Post